Wealth Magic

Wealth Magic

From **broke** to **Multi-Millionaire** in just **7** years

Peter Spann

HarperCollins*Publishers*

HarperCollins*Publishers*

First published in Australia in 2001
Reprinted in 2001 (twice)
by HarperCollins*Publishers* Pty Limited
ABN 36 009 913 517
A member of the HarperCollins*Publishers* (Australia) Pty Limited Group
www.harpercollins.com.au

Copyright © Peter Spann 2001

The right of Peter Spann to be identified as the moral rights
author of this work has been asserted by him in accordance
with the *Copyright Amendment (Moral Rights) Act 2000* (Cth).

HarperCollins*Publishers*
25 Ryde Road, Pymble, Sydney, NSW 2073, Australia
31 View Road, Glenfield, Auckland 10, New Zealand
77–85 Fulham Palace Road, London, W6 8JB, United Kingdom
Hazelton Lanes, 55 Avenue Road, Suite 2900, Toronto, Ontario M5R 3L2
and 1995 Markham Road, Scarborough, Ontario M1B 5M8, Canada
10 East 53rd Street, New York NY 10022, USA

National Library of Australia Cataloguing-in-Publication data:

Spann, Peter.
  Wealth magic.
  ISBN 0 7322 7431 1.
  1. Spann, Peter. 2. Finance, Personal – Australia.
  3. Investments – Australia. I. Title.
332.02400994

Cover photo of author by Scott Cameron
Cover design by Nick Foote, HarperCollins Design Studio
Typeset by HarperCollins in 11/14 Sabon
Printed and bound in Australia by Griffin Press on 79gsm Bulky Paperback White

8 7 6 5 4 3   01 02 03 04

Dedicated to dreams — may they always come true. Most of all though, this book is dedicated to Leisl Baker, my beautiful friend, who through her support, loyalty, dedication, love and inspiration, helped make my dream a reality.

Contents

Preface

This is unashamedly a tale of rags to riches.

It starts at a point in my life where I was borderline destitute, owing way more money than I had or could even dream of accessing, and takes you through to a time in my life when my net worth was in the many millions of dollars. And along the way, it gives you timeless advice in how you can emulate this success.

It might help you to know that I am not a particularly special person. I grew up in a nice, middle-class family where we lived an OK life but my father was always struggling to make ends meet. I didn't do particularly well at school, and still can't do maths unless I have a calculator.

As a teenager I took the path of rebellion and started getting myself into all manner of strife. If you can imagine it, I probably did it. I was in strife with my school, which I managed to get expelled from, and the deputy principal commented that I would "amount to nothing". I was in strife with the law. And later, when I graduated from university with a B.A., I was in strife with my employers, who fired me from just about every job I held.

I was in monetary strife as well. After failing to hold down any decent job, I had started a business. It was a little toyshop, which had started out as a "great idea" but ended up being a resounding failure so, at the age of 22, I found myself bankrupt.

With my history, there weren't many people on the face of the planet who had much faith in me. But with the assistance of the few who did, and with some skills and knowledge I will share with you in this book, as well as a bit of grit and determination,

I managed to claw my way up and up. In a mere seven years, I would be rewarded with more material wealth than I could have imagined when this story begins.

I hope my story helps you understand that, no matter where you are now, it *is* possible for you to become wealthy. If you are as badly off as I was when I began, this story should give you the encouragement and support you need to start. If you are better off than I was, then you know that you can start where you are and succeed with even more speed than me by using my strategy.

Either way, if I can do it, so can you.

Success

To laugh often and much, to win the respect of intelligent people and the affection of children, to earn the appreciation of honest critics and endure the betrayal of false friends, to appreciate beauty, to find the best in others, to leave the world a bit better, whether by a healthy child, a garden patch or redeemed social condition, to know that one life has breathed easier because you have lived. This is to have succeeded.

Ralph Waldo Emerson

CHAPTER 1

In Which Life is Miserable

Growing up I dreamt of being rich.

I used to watch TV shows and read magazines that had me salivating at the lifestyles of the wealthy. They fuelled my dreams of riches.

And yet at the age of 22, despite all my best efforts and the time I'd spent at university, I found myself deeply in debt, working as a part-time check-out operator at a supermarket, earning $4.72 an hour.

I was bankrupt and owed about $160,000, and couldn't even list my address anywhere just in case the debt collectors caught up with me, so I had to live in a condemned house.

Water dripped on my bed when it rained and there was no hot water. My housemates and I used to boil up water on a gas BBQ and put it into a camp shower when we wanted to wash.

I lived for three weeks on "No Name Brand" canned tuna that was out of date and reduced in price by 70% from the supermarket.

Perhaps, compared to some people, my life wasn't that bad. But at the time I thought it sucked.

With failure after failure in my life, prospects were not looking good. Sometimes I couldn't even afford a bus fare to visit my beautiful friend, and my fortnightly pay packet ran out long before a fortnight.

For some reason people seem to treat check-out operators really badly, so there were days when I woke up in tears and could hardly drag myself out of bed I was so depressed.

— $$$ —

Eventually I saved enough to buy a little car. It was a Leyland Marina, painted white with house paint (you could see patches of baby-poo yellow underneath), with a red vinyl interior. It cost me $400, which included 12 months' registration. It ran on just three of its four cylinders and used so much oil that my beautiful friend and I called it "Saddam" because you needed Kuwait to run it.

Oil poured out at such a rate we chicken-wired a baking tray under the motor to collect the oil. When the red warning light came on, we simply pulled over, dragged out the baking tray and poured the oil back into the motor with a funnel, and kept on driving. Saddam would overheat, needed to be clutch started and didn't like the rain, but it got us around.

Sometimes I escaped the condemned house and stayed at my beautiful friend's place. One cold, wet winter's morning she woke me up. She was running late and had missed her train — could I drive her to work? Relying on Saddam was always going to be risky, but to attempt such a perilous journey in this weather... well, that was plain lunacy.

Seeing, however, that she was so dear to me, I thought I should tender some assistance.

There was not enough time to dress so I simply pulled a coat over my PJs and ran out to the car.

Everything was going well until we got to the "killer hill". This hill had a set of traffic lights at the top. For some reason Saddam would stop running if it had to stop in traffic while facing up or down a hill. In light traffic this wouldn't be a problem, you would simply let the car roll forwards or backwards, pop the clutch and away you'd go, but in heavy traffic you had to hope that the lights stayed green.

I had just started to read positive-thinking books and had come to believe that, if I remained positive, I might just be able to influence things such as traffic lights. So, with a great degree of earnestness and concentration, my beautiful friend and I were shouting out, "Green! Green! Green!" all the way up the hill.

My heart sank as the light turned yellow, but there was still time to get through...

Well, the car in front stopped and we stopped too.

And Saddam conked out, billowing smoke and steam, never to start again.

My beautiful friend did the only intelligent thing she could, and took off, leaving me to accept the abuse heaped on me by my fellow motorists as I blocked their progress to their work in peak-hour traffic.

Nobody stopped to help.

Fed up, I crawled up onto the top of the car and sat down, giving "the fork" to anybody who stared at me. Soon I was soaking wet, with only my coat and flannelette pyjamas to shield me from the rain. The police, when they came, tried to coax me down, convinced I'd gone insane — and in a way, I had.

I had reached the point of no return.

At that moment I was so disgusted in myself, so angry at how bleak I had allowed my life to become, so miserable, I simply could take it no longer.

It was at that moment that I vowed to myself that I would *never* allow myself to be this low again. And I vowed that I would one day be a multi-millionaire. I marked that day in my calendar as the first day, as they say, of the rest of my life.

Little did I suspect that the first million would come so soon.

Lesson

You are in charge of your destiny.

CHAPTER 2

In Which I Consult a Wealthy Friend

I knew that being a check-out operator wasn't going to make me wealthy. So I started to think who I could ask for advice.

My father was a pensioner and renowned for passing up opportunities that other people had turned into gold. My friends all had jobs and, even though they were earning more than me, they seemed just as miserable and still couldn't make ends meet.

The only really wealthy person I knew was a friend's father. I knew he often drank coffee at an expensive café a few suburbs from where I lived, so I got on the bus and went over there hoping to find him.

When I arrived at the café it was just opening for business and only a few people were there, quietly reading their morning papers and getting their caffeine fix. I waited at a table near the window.

After a few hours his gold Rolls Royce pulled up at the curb, his chauffeur opened the door, and he headed for his usual table.

When I first approached him I think he thought I was a beggar — and I guess, compared to the stylishly dressed people around me, I did look a bit shoddy — but as soon as I told him that I knew his daughter, he smiled and asked me to join him.

We talked for a long time about this and that, and eventually I had the opportunity to ask the question that was burning inside me: "How do I get rich?"

"How do you get rich?" he repeated, surprised by the question.

"Umm, yes, I want to know how to be successful."

"Well, that's a different question. Which do you want?"

I had never thought that you could be rich without being successful and vice versa, and he obviously could tell by my hesitation that I couldn't discern between the two.

"'Rich'," he said, "is just when you have a lot of money. That's all. 'Successful' is when you are doing what you love and love what you do, when you're surrounded by those you love, and you are rewarded in a manner that suits you."

"So you don't need to be rich to be successful?" I asked.

"Nope, you could actually have no money at all."

Suddenly that didn't sound so appealing, and so I said, "I guess I want to be rich then."

"Don't they all?" he quipped, and then took a long sip of his cappuccino. "And how will you know when you are rich?"

I wasn't expecting all these questions, but I thought for a second and had a brainwave: "I'll be a millionaire!"

"Well, at least that's a start. You see, Peter," he went on, "most people have no idea of what they *actually* want. They have vague notions of wanting to be 'rich' or 'successful' or 'wealthy', but they never take the time out to define exactly what that will be for them.

"Each person has an entirely different view of wealth and success. And it's important for you to remember that your view is equally as valid as somebody else's. My idea of wealth will not be yours, and your idea of wealth will not be mine. People allow themselves to be influenced far too much by what other people think, instead of exercising their brains and deciding for themselves.

"The human mind is like a heat-seeking missile that will seek out a target with precision, ducking and weaving around obstacles and remain focused no matter how many manoeuvres the target does. And goals can seem like a target — always doing everything they can to escape you. But without a target, your missile will just float around in the atmosphere with nowhere to go. Unfortunately, most people live like this. They haven't set strong targets for themselves, so they don't know what to do or even when they have achieved it.

"Do you even know what a million dollars looks like, Peter?"

I had to admit I didn't. I had an idea, though — I imagined Scrooge McDuck swimming around in his money bin. How fabulous that would be, I thought.

"Well, Peter, it's your lucky day. I am prepared to help you understand and reach your goal, but only on a few conditions...

"One, that you are prepared to do some work — to carry out the tasks that I set you.

"Two, that you will see it through to the end.

"Three, that you will not waste my time by not preparing for our meetings.

"And four, that, when you do indeed meet your goal, you will share what you learn with others."

"OK," I said eagerly.

"Are you sure?" he said with an ominous tone I hadn't expected.

"Yes, I'm sure."

And so he set me my very first task (the first of many to come): *to find out what a million dollars looks like.*

"Is that all?" I asked, obviously disappointed.

"Why, what were you expecting?"

"I don't know, a hot stock-tip or something."

"Peter, there is no quick-fix way to wealth. People are forever chasing get-rich-quick schemes, looking for the big hit — it doesn't exist — it's Lotto mentality. Wealthy people get that way through a thorough understanding of the processes of wealth. It takes time, effort, knowledge and energy. If you really want to become wealthy, I'm happy to teach you; but, as I said, don't waste my time if you're not prepared to put in the effort."

Suddenly my audience was over. My wealthy friend wanted to settle in and read the finance pages of the newspaper, no doubt to check how much his wealth had risen overnight. He wrote down a telephone number on a paper napkin, and passed it to me. "You can reach me on that number. Ring me when you have finished your task."

I must admit, I left our meeting feeling quite frustrated. I had expected the secret to life, the Universe and everything, and all I got was this seemingly useless task.

I felt like I should get one of those T-shirts that say, "I had coffee with a multi-millionaire and all I got was this dumb task." But remembering his Rolex watch and the platinum card with which he paid for his coffee reminded me that he must know something about money, so I decided to carry out his task.

Finding someone to show me a million dollars was harder than I thought. I mean, who carries around a million dollars?

After much talk, finally I convinced a bank manager to let me see what a million looked like on the proviso I did it on a pre-arranged tour with a group of other people. That certainly didn't seem unreasonable and I relished the opportunity of sharing a tour with people who would no doubt be high-powered business executives, maybe even Arab sheiks!

On the night before the appointed day, I could hardly sleep. I lay awake for hours, thinking about the size of the vault and the bars and locks and laser beams that would be there to protect it. Imagine, *me* standing next to a million dollars, I thought. I finally drifted off to sleep with pictures of me swimming in all that lovely loot and wondering if they'd actually let me keep some as a souvenir of my day at the bank.

I got up early next morning and dressed in my best clothes (which weren't that fabulous, but they were my best). I looked around at the condemned house that I was living in and observed the squalor of it all.

My housemates were not fabulous at cleaning up — there didn't seem much point in a condemned house — and the house always had a strange odour of mould and old socks.

All of a sudden I was hit with a genuine sense that I'd soon be out of there and that this day at the bank with a million dollars would make all the difference.

I turned up early, not wanting to miss the tour, and told the manager I was there. He seemed quite blasé about my introduction to the million, and asked me to sit in a small, hot reception area that seemed to lack the air-conditioning that the rest of the building had. The other people were waiting to see the loans officers of the bank. "I think they are trying to make us sweat," said one.

All of a sudden the bank was filled with a commotion. A gaggle of five-year-olds burst onto the scene in a fit of noise and activity that had their teacher in a pickle as she tried to keep them all under control. They were obviously excited about something, but I was irritated that they had interrupted my "special day" and my dreams of swimming in money.

The bank manger came out and beckoned for me and the teacher to follow. Once the teacher had the kids in some semblance of control, they screamed and screeched and played their way behind us.

'Was *this* my tour group?' I thought in dismay. This day wasn't turning out to be special at all.

The bank manger, in a rather uninspiring drawl, showed us all the aspects of life in a bank, giving the kids a turn at pushing some buttons on an adding machine and watching the cheques zip though franking machines. By the time we got to the staff lunch-room, my frustration was mounting.

"OK, kids," he said, obviously winding up to some big event, "are you ready to see the money?"

They all signalled their readiness by getting even more excited.

At last we get to see the vault, I thought.

"We just have to wait for security," he said with a dramatic flair that looked promising.

I imagined big burly guys, fit as body builders, armed to the hilt, accompanied by trained Alsatians straining at the leash, fangs ready to rip to shreds anyone threatening the loot.

I must say that when "security" finally turned up, I was under-whelmed.

He was fat, had a stain on his shirt from an over-vigorous indulgence at meal time, and was wearing one of those silly caps (which he kept removing to scratch his bald patch). There wasn't a dog in sight, and his only weapon seemed to be an old torch strapped to his belt with a combination of leather and plumber's tape.

This wasn't turning out even remotely like I expected it.

The security guard waddled towards what looked like a steel door, nothing like I imagined the massive vault to be, and opened it with a simple set of keys he had attached to his belt.

I fought off a few five-year-olds — mostly the girls, some of those guys were tough — to get as close as possible to the front of the line to see the money.

"Well," said the bank manager encouragingly, "here it is, one million dollars!"

The boys at the front of the line seemed somewhat uninterested, one going back to his portable video game within seconds of giving the money a glance. I maintained my excitement, however, as the kids slowly shuffled past in the first moments of silence they had exhibited since arriving at the bank.

Finally it was my turn, and there it was: one million dollars.

Surprisingly it didn't gleam like I'd expected it to, and the pile of money was smaller than I had expected — much, much smaller. In actual fact it was about 60 centimetres square. Less than even a cubic metre. Smaller than a tea-chest. You certainly couldn't bathe in it, much less go for a swim in it.

"Is that all?" I asked out loud.

"Why yes," replied the bank manager. "Impressive, isn't it?"

I looked around at the vault in case I had missed something. I didn't want to be rude and say it hadn't impressed me at all. In fact, if a million was only that much, I wondered why it was so hard to get.

After the vault was closed we endured the bank manager's thank-you speech and were all given little steel money boxes in the shape of a small bank. With a flourish, he put 50 cents in each box as he handed it to us as "the start to our million dollars", compliments of the bank.

Well, at least one thing I had dreamt of came true — we certainly got to keep some of the money! (I think that was the first and only money a bank has ever given me for free!)

I had completed the task and it was time to go back to my wealthy friend.

Lesson

"Rich" is just when you have a lot of money. "Successful" is when you are doing what you love and love what you do, when you're surrounded by those you love, and you are rewarded in a manner that suits you.

There is no quick-fix way to wealth. It takes time, effort, knowledge and energy.

CHAPTER 3

In Which I Get Something to Aim For

I called the number my wealthy friend had written for me on the napkin of the café where we first met. I thought it strange that he didn't have a business card.

A pleasant-sounding woman answered the phone and told me that my wealthy friend was away at a spa that week but he would be happy to see me on his return, and she made an appointment for me to meet him at his office.

In the ensuing week, I commented to my manager at the supermarket that I had gone to considerable effort to see a million dollars and was, in summary, unimpressed. "It's just not as much as I thought it was."

He laughed and said, "Why didn't you ask me? We put a million dollars through here each week. Haven't you seen the security trucks pull up to collect it?"

I started to look at the amount of money that I put through even my own cash register, and realised that I would have seen a million dollars every few weeks.

At last the day arrived to meet my wealthy friend at his office. I went to the 35th floor of one of the biggest buildings in the city, and the woman attached to the pleasant voice directed me to sit on a deep, comfortable leather sofa. As I looked around the reception area, I was amazed by the beautiful collection of paintings and sculptures and just the pure space of what appeared to be the reception area for my wealthy friend's office only. I couldn't help but imagine how much rent he would be paying for so much space.

As I looked out over the stunning view from the panoramic windows, I spotted a distant helicopter coming towards the building. I watched it with amusement as it went from a tiny speck to my being able to see the faces of the pilots. I was suddenly alarmed as I realised they were coming straight for me. At the last minute it swooped up and disappeared out of my view, but I could still hear the rotor blades as the helicopter landed, obviously on the roof of the building.

Less than a minute later, my wealthy friend appeared. I thought for a moment about the difference in the ways we both got to work — him arriving in style in a private helicopter — me arriving in a billow of smoke and a sea of dripping oil in Saddam.

"Good to see you again," he said, putting out his hand for me to shake and guiding me to a chair near a beautifully carved, round wooden table in front of his desk. "What did you think of the million dollars?"

"To tell you the truth," I replied, "not much. I thought it would have been much more impressive."

"I thought as much," he said, sipping on a drink whisked in by the pleasant woman as a glass of fresh, cold water was placed next to me.

"Most people think a million is a lot of money, but in reality it isn't. It's been built up as if it's a lot, so people think it's hard to get. While ever people think a million is a lot, it's unlikely that they will ever become millionaires, and if they do they are likely to stop there because they now think they have heaps. But they don't. At bank interest, a million will provide less every year than most people are capable of earning at even relatively simple jobs. If you're going to be rich, you're going to want a lot more than that."

I nodded in agreement.

"But, no matter how much you actually want, it's more important to know what you want to do with it. Have you heard the song 'If I Had a Million Dollars'?" Without waiting for my reply, he went on, "It's all about what the person singing the song would do with the million dollars, not about the money itself. Who ever wrote that song was on the right track.

"You see, it's pretty hard to keep yourself motivated if all you think about is money. And while it's good to set yourself a target, it's more important for you to come up with a purpose for the money and focus on everything you'd do with it."

"Well, for starters," I said, "I'd buy myself a decent car!"

My wealthy friend just laughed and went on, "It's those things, opportunities, and contributions that will keep you going and keep you interested in making money. The money itself is unimportant. What's important is what you are going to *do* with it. Money *and* something worthwhile to do with it. And *that's* success!"

"I want you to go home and think about what you would do if you became rich. What you would spend your money on, what opportunities you would explore, and what contributions you would make. Make it into a list. And when you've made the list, go over it again and again to make sure what you have written down really means something to you. Revise it until you have a concise list of things, opportunities and contributions that really appeal to you. This list will become your reasons and it will propel you to wealth quicker than any strategy I can give you.

"When you've done all that, I want you to write a description of what you will do on the day you become rich. How you will celebrate, who you will be with, and what you'll be doing.

"And finally, when you've done that, call me and I will tell you about the Key to Wealth.

Now I was excited. All the possibilities started to flood in.

I went to a newsagency and bought some magazines on lavish lifestyles, and cut out pictures of what appealed to me. I went to a remainder bookshop and bought some coffee-table books on beautiful houses and expensive cars and boats, and desecrated them by cutting them up, extracting the pictures that most appealed to me, and I came up with my list.

It included a heap of things ... cars, boats, houses, holidays with friends and family, the charities I was going to donate to, the people I would employ, and the lifestyle I would lead.

I was enthusiastic to be planning this exciting life. I had no idea how I was going to get it — but the mere thought that I might be able to encouraged me no end.

And then I had to plan my celebration day. I decided to enlist the help of my beautiful friend. She had more exposure to lavish lifestyles than I did and was always good to talk things through with.

We talked and talked and talked, and I had more fun in those few hours that I'd had in years. It was exciting and silly all at the same time, as we worked through all the possibilities.

But finally I decided that the ultimate glamour town was Monte Carlo. Its beautiful yachts, shops, people and Grand Casino had featured in just about every book, magazine, TV show and movie I had ever seen about the rich and famous. I had fallen in love with Ferraris while watching the TV show *Miami Vice* and so I decided we'd have to arrive in a bright red one. My beautiful friend was determined not to be left out.

"I'm going with you," she said, "and I'm going to be wearing a $10,000 dress!"

"Sounds good to me," I said, and went to sleep that night dreaming of this amazing future.

Lesson

The money itself is unimportant. What's important is what you are going to *do* with it. Money *and* something worthwhile to do with it. And *that's* success!

CHAPTER 4

The Key to Wealth

"So, what is the Key to Wealth?" I asked.

My wealthy friend's answer was so simple, it almost escaped me. At the time I didn't realise how profound it was, and when you read it in just a moment, you too may be tempted to dismiss it as too simple or too obvious. But as I have become wealthier and wealthier over the years, I have discovered that it is the simple things that are most often overlooked.

Take a look at the lives of successful people — people who are not only rich but happy too.

Their lives seem simple. They don't seem to work *that* hard (although obviously work is necessary if you are going to become rich). They seem to be able to fit in enough time for work, family, play and friends. They are constantly presented heaps of opportunities and offers, but seem to stick to what they know and can do well. They have discovered that simple things done well, done with passion and done often, are the most rewarding, both financially and personally.

And so in my ignorant and non-educated state I was all too ready to dismiss the simple wisdom that was offered to me, and yet it has stayed with me throughout my life as the one, only and most undeniable Key to Wealth.

"Knowledge," he said. "That is the Key to Wealth."

"Is that it?"

"Yes," he replied. Sensing my disappointment (again), he went on: "It's not just knowledge but what you do with it. Every day people are ripped off and defrauded, misadvised and misled, simply because they lack knowledge. And this is no more prevalent than in the area of money.

"Every day you can read a sob story in a newspaper where somebody lost their money through a get-rich scheme that they would never have become involved in if they'd had knowledge. You lost your money in your business because you didn't have enough knowledge to make it a success."

Well, that was certainly true.

"You could have made that business a success, but you didn't take the time to assess your skills, to know where your strengths lay and where you had gaps and holes in your knowledge. If you had taken the time to recognise your lack of knowledge, you could have done the study to find the answers to the problems presented in your business.

"People get paid for their knowledge. They go to school, and then go through training courses and apprenticeships to acquire knowledge so they can get jobs for pay. If they know how to build a house, they get paid. If they know how to run a business, they get paid. If they know how to nurse or teach, they get paid. But people forget the fundamental rule that it is their knowledge that they get paid for, so they stop learning. They forget that when they got a skill and learnt how to apply it, their pay and their wealth went up. They get too busy to keep on learning and applying new knowledge.

"What can you do?" he asked.

The only answer I could come up with was: "Well, not much at this stage. I have too many problems in my life."

"And *there* is your problem. You will never be wealthy with that attitude. There is no problem that has not already had a solution found for it; no idea that has not had a way to come into reality; no success strategy that has not already been discovered, tried, tested and perfected, that has not been recorded somewhere. All that knowledge is just waiting for you to learn and to apply.

"Each great business, each great product, each great income-producing asset started in somebody's head as an idea. Look at the wealthiest people in the world. They have invested in their own or other people's ideas — they applied knowledge. The businesses that have made them such a success, the investments that have done so well for them, were all ideas in somebody's head that were thought through and then brought into reality through applied knowledge.

"The key is: they started with something that they could do well, and was interesting enough to them that they were able to stick at it and find a way to be rewarded for doing it.

"Not only did they develop their knowledge into a skill, they developed it into a love, so they were able to focus on it with joy virtually every waking moment of the day. They loved their idea so much they were prepared to protect it when it was attacked, nurture it and watch it grow, work on it, with it, and recruit people to help with it and never give up on it, no matter how tough things got. They were so excited about their idea, everything they did to make it into reality was so much fun they had to keep doing it. They were so enthusiastic about their idea, and so persistent in its selling, it became contagious, and other people got infected and interested in it.

"Knowledge applied is the Key to Wealth.

"Fall in love with knowledge, learn how to apply your ideas in a way that people will reward you for it, and wealth will become inevitable for you."

It was time to assess my skills.

Lesson

There is no problem that has not already had a solution found for it; no idea that has not had a way to come into reality; no success strategy that has not already been discovered, tried, tested and perfected, that has not been recorded somewhere. All that knowledge is just waiting for you to learn and apply.

Knowledge applied is the Key to Wealth.

CHAPTER 5

In Which a Plan is Hatched and Dashed

I started to think about my skills.

Even though I'd gone broke when my retail business had failed, other shop owners and business people had frequently commented how good my marketing was. I seemed to have a flair for it. Not only that, it was something I enjoyed doing and had been rewarded for when I was a teenager and passionate about the theatre. In those days, I used to sell advertising in theatre programs to raise enough funds to produce plays and I would write the ads myself. While I doubt if any of the business people who bought my ads became rich on the sales my ads produced, they all commented that they liked the fact I wasn't just hitting them for a donation.

I wondered if I couldn't get a job doing that.

I started to read everything I could about marketing and advertising. I couldn't afford to enrol in a course or buy books, but I could afford a library card, and so I learnt that what you need to become rich is often available for free.

I wrote dozens and dozens of letters to ad agencies, telling them how good I was and asking for a job. I would look in newspapers and see companies' ads and re-write them, re-design them and send them off to their marketing departments as examples of my work. Then I sat back, expecting job offers to come pouring in. Occasionally I'd get an interview.

I couldn't afford a new suit, so I went to the local op shop and found the best suit I could for $2. It was dark blue with a wide grey pinstripe. (I imagine that at some stage it would have been quite stylish! I still have that suit, and I'm waiting for the time when it will come back into style.) I bought a white shirt on special from the supermarket for $7 and the most conservative tie I could find on the $5 rack.

So off I would go to my interview, in my $14 outfit, panicking all the time because of the hours I was giving up at the supermarket and thinking about how I was going to pay the bills when my pay packet was reduced for time off without pay.

I would nervously wait my turn in the line to be interviewed and then summarily dismissed with the traditional lines: "You don't have any experience", "We want somebody older, younger, bigger, smaller, cuter..." And I'd slink back to my supermarket register just a little bit sorrier and with just a little less self-esteem.

My plan to become rich through the advertising game was quickly becoming yet another dashed dream.

It was time to consult my wealthy friend.

Lesson

I couldn't afford to enrol in a course or buy books, but I could afford a library card, and so I learnt that what you need to become rich is often available for free.

CHAPTER 6

The Key to Success

"Trying too hard," he said.

"What? Didn't you say I should get attached to my idea and persist at it?"

"Yes, but not desperately obsessed with it — people can smell the desperation on you."

That's more likely to be the dank smell from my $2 suit, I thought to myself, suddenly distracted from the lesson I was getting.

"You need to relax."

"You see," he said, going slower now because I obviously didn't understand, "knowledge is the Key to Wealth, but if you are going to be successful, you need another key."

"There are two keys?" I asked, beginning to doubt my friend.

"One Key to Wealth, one Key to Success.

"When we come into contact with other human beings, we transmit subtle signals as to how we are feeling, what we are thinking, and how we are reacting. These signals are unconscious and are picked up unconsciously at the same time.

"Have you ever been to a party and seen someone coming towards you, and even though you have never met them, and don't know them, you form an instant attraction or dislike for them?"

"Of course," I said, remembering my track record with women at parties, "that must be why women stay away from me," I joked, not expecting his response.

"Exactly!"

"Obviously you are putting out the same signals at job interviews as you are at parties!"

I was expecting more encouragement.

"What you put out is what you get back — that's the Key to Success."

"All living things are made up of tiny atoms buzzing around and held together by an electromagnetic field. The way you feel, what you are thinking, and your intentions, all affect the level of activity of your atoms. This in turn interacts with the atmosphere around you, causing those atoms to respond. If you are in a good or bad mood, this is transmitted to the atmosphere and interacts with other people as they come into your 'space'. They pick up on your mood and sometimes are even affected by it.

"And it works on many levels, not just subtle signals to people in your close vicinity. The mood that you have, the thoughts that you harbour and the desires you hold are transmitted out all around you. People, things and resources are attracted to other people who are putting out the same signals they are. Depressed people seem to be attracted to other depressed people, happy people hang around with other happy people. People like people who are like them.

"What you put out is what you get. If you are nervous about life, this is transmitted out to the people around you and they pick up on those subtle signals. Even though you might have a great idea and you are passionate about it, people are not going to want to help you with it if the signals you are giving out are not positive."

I had to stop him for a minute. "Hey," I retorted, "this sounds like that positive-thinking stuff. I tried that with the traffic light, and it didn't work!"

"To a certain degree it is about being positive, but it is much more than that. The more you put out there, the more ideas you have, the more enthusiastic you are, the more attractive and interesting you become. People like hanging around with attractive and interesting people. Eventually, if you do it enough, somebody will become interested enough in you to give you a break. Why don't you start at work?"

"Huh?"

"Your work, you have a job don't you?"

"But I work as a check-out operator in a supermarket! You hardly expect me to become interested in that, do you — it's a miserable job."

"It's miserable," he said, suddenly frustrated at my ignorance, "because you make it miserable."

"There are many people who would love to have the job you do, interacting with people, getting out and about, seeing products and having fun."

He obviously had no idea what a check-out operator actually did.

"Look," he said, and I sensed that the conversation was coming to an end, "you want to be in marketing don't you?"

"A-huh."

"Well, it's about time you started marketing yourself. It seems to me that marketing is a combination of sales and service. Start with your job. Learn how to sell, learn how to serve — build your knowledge. And do it with a smile on your face. Remember, what you put out — you get back."

Lesson

What you put out is what you get back — that is the Key to Success.

CHAPTER 7

In Which Some Progress is Made

Service and selling. I was sceptical that this would make a difference to anything. How could I do that standing behind a register? But mindful of my wealthy friend's advice that what you give out you get back, I decided to give it a go.

I read about customer service and started to notice how bad it was in the businesses where I spent my meagre funds.

And I started to think about how I was marketing myself and the job I had.

While my job was not fulfilling my ambitions for employment, I *was* grateful that I had a job. I decided that if they were the only people who were prepared to employ me, I would become the best check-out operator ever.

I started smiling, chatting to people and sorting groceries properly into bags, making sure there was never too much in there so the bags wouldn't break. I bought packets of small lollies, put them in a jar and gave them out to customers, thanking them for coming through my line.

I read in a book about a person in a similar job who typed up daily quotes and handed them out, so I did the same.

I noticed how successful McDonald's seemed to be with that little question, "Would you like some fries with that?" and so I started collecting things from around the store that I thought people would buy, putting them in trays next to my register and selling them to people as they came through. My check out started to resemble a little jumble sale, with baskets stacked up wherever I could put them. My supervisor had hysterics because it all looked so messy!

I wrote notes on what in the store seemed to be extra fresh or particularly interesting, and I would think of ways I could help people. I'd say things like, "I notice you have some ice cream — did you know that we have some delicious fresh strawberries that are on special this week?" I'd then stop what I was doing and call somebody from fruit and veg to bring them over for the customer.

All of a sudden the job became just a little bit better.

People were often still rude, despite my best efforts, but the time went quicker and I started to enjoy life a little bit more. The other check-out operators regarded me with suspicion, and my supervisor certainly didn't like the fact that I had slowed down my scan rate (the number of items you scan in a minute was regarded as one of the performance indicators by the store), and the odd customer complained that I was way too slow.

I even got counselled by the store manager, but I was sure that my approach of offering exceptional customer service would pay off and continued to do my little tricks and schemes to get people smiling and buying.

My wealthy friend called me one day and asked me how it was going. When I told him, he said, "That should be your motto: 'Keep the customer smiling and buying.'" And so I did.

When my supervisor came over to chip me about how slow my scanning was, I'd just say to her, "Smiling and buying." She would grunt something at me about my being an imbecile and eventually give up in despair. I guess I was lucky that they needed check-out operators!

I still sent off letters asking for jobs, and still held hope that one day I would get a response, but nothing came. I couldn't figure it out. I was putting out all the good "vibes" I could muster, and nothing much seemed to be coming back except complaints from my supervisor!

"Keep at it," my wealthy friend said, calling on the mobile phone from his Rolls Royce.

Eventually my boss *did* notice the job I was doing. One day he saw a dozen people standing in my line while only two or three people were in the other lines. He stormed up, demanding to know what was taking so long to get my customers through.

"Smiling and buying," I said.

He wanted to know what I was on about, and so I suggested he ask the people queuing in my line. I had noticed a couple of "regulars" and hoped they would help me.

So he asked a couple of customers why they were waiting in my queue, and they said, "Because we like dealing with Peter so much." That people would wait patiently in one line while other lines moved quicker had never occurred in the history of the supermarket.

The next day he caught me as I was picking up my pay. "Peter," he said, "I checked your performance indicators, and even though your scan rate is very slow, the average basket is much higher through your register, in fact, your register is the most profitable we have in the store! Good job!"

Pity I wasn't on commission.

I noticed how much different my attitude was, now that I seemed happy to serve. I thought back to the days when I was stuck in my own shop, hating every minute and viewing the odd customer that did get up the courage to enter as an interruption to my misery at having to be there.

I wondered what would have happened if, when I had my own shop, I'd had the knowledge I had now.

Heck knows, I'd certainly had enough time to gain the knowledge, sitting there waiting for customers. Instead of spending my time in the mall whingeing with the other shopkeepers about how lousy business was — and complaining how the horrible kids who came into my store constantly got my stock dirty and how I wished they wouldn't come in! — I could have been reading, learning and growing.

And instead of complaining about all the "lookers" who came into my store and never bought anything, I wondered what would have happened if I had spent the time with them "smiling and buying" just as I had in the supermarket.

It now occurred to me to work out how much more I would have needed to sell to make the business viable, and it shocked me to discover I would have only needed $35 a day more to break even. Sheesh, I was personally selling more than that every *hour* just standing at my cash register!

I learnt a lot about marketing from the kids who came into our supermarket with their mothers.

They would pick something up and ask if they could have it. More often than not, their mothers said "No". That didn't seem to perturb them though. They would just wait for another opportunity. It amazed me that no matter what happened — getting yelled at, smacked, threatened, or ignored — they would *always* ask again. And again. And again. And again. Until finally, the mothers relented and gave the kids what they wanted.

It astonished me that such little beings could constantly outwit and outsmart their adult "prey" to such a level that they always got what they wanted.

I tried it myself. If somebody wouldn't sample my lovely strawberries (or mangoes or whatever I had in my baskets that day), I would simply get on with my scanning until I saw another opportunity. "Come on," I would encourage, "they're yummy!" until they would try. Most of the time they would also buy. But if they didn't, I still wouldn't let them get away without one more try. At the very end, when I had finished everything and pressed sub-total, I would put a big smile on my face and ask, "Are you sure you wouldn't like to take these home with you?" And very often people would smile back and hand over the additional 70 cents for their punnet.

I wondered when it was that we forgot this simple skill of selling.

So sell I did, at every opportunity.

And I would see my manager walk past, see the people lined up behind my register, and smile.

I got promoted. First to full-time check out operator. Finally a regular income. And then to department manager, and my first pay rise.

What I was putting out certainly seemed to be coming back to me. Maybe my wealthy friend was right after all. I told him this and he just laughed, brushing me off to go back to his golf.

Yet I was still sending out application after application for the job I had decided I would love — marketing.

And still, no offers came.

Time to get serious.

Lesson

Progress is made only with a skill applied and persistence.

CHAPTER 8

In Which an Opportunity and a Problem are Presented at Once

At last, an ad that said the magic words: "No experience required."

A small consulting company was looking for a trainee copywriter. They were only offering a small wage, even less than I was now earning at the supermarket, but it could be my big break.

I decided to pull something out of the hat. I sent a picture of myself with a caption that said: "This man is so sure you will love his work, he is prepared to work for a month for free!" It got me the interview.

As it turned out, the owner of the company had written a book that I had read and so I was able to talk to him about that. Impressed with my enthusiasm and obvious confidence, but concerned about my lack of skills (funny how when they say "no experience necessary" they still want you to have experience!), he decided to take me up on my one month free trial offer.

But now I had a problem — I couldn't actually afford to work for free. I had only just got in front of my bills, and the car had broken down yet again. If I worked for nothing for a month, I would be broke again.

My wealthy friend seemed positively excited when I called him for help this time. "Excellent," he said. "Every major opportunity is always presented with a problem. It's a test to make sure that you are really committed to your idea.

"Many people fail to take up the opportunity because all they see is the problem. Instead of finding a way to overcome the problem and get on with the opportunity, they get stuck with the problem. Remember, what you put out you get back, so when you focus on the problem you can no longer see the opportunity. People then wonder why they don't get many opportunities and start questioning their idea."

I was about to ask more but he terminated the conversation, keen to get onto his yacht and go sailing, by saying, "This is telling you that you're on the right track — congratulations. Just focus on the opportunity and find a way to overcome the problem."

I accepted the job and got to start on Monday, but still had to give one month's notice at the supermarket.

How was I going to do two jobs at once, I wondered. There was only one course of action: 'fess up to the boss and ask for his help.

"I guess we were lucky to have you for this long," the supermarket manager said, "but I can't get you out of your notice period — you'll just have to start with the new company later."

I knew by the way my new employer had said "I *need* you to start on Monday" this would not be negotiable.

I went home that night disappointed and despondent. Finally I had got a break and by a cruel twist of fate I couldn't take advantage of it. But I remembered the little children and their mothers, and decided to persist.

Next day I was back in the manager's office. "Surely there's a way I can work out my notice and still start at this other job on Monday?"

The supermarket manager sat down and applied his brain to the problem. "Well," he said, "the night stacking manager just left and we need somebody in there until we can find a replacement, but that would mean you'd be working all day *and* all night."

"Excellent," I said, "I'll start tonight!"

Working 20 hours a day was a unique experience. I was dead tired, but with this new job I was "alive" at work for the first time in my life. I was doing something that I was not only good at, but which I enjoyed as well.

I counted the days I had to work at the supermarket and on my last day I walked out, without fanfare, never to return.

I often wonder what happened to the people I worked with in that supermarket and shared a year with. The sassy girls with dreams of a better life. I hope they got their hopes and dreams. They deserved them ... we all do.

Lesson

Every major opportunity is always presented with a problem. It's a test to make sure that you are really committed to your idea. Just focus on the opportunity and find a way to overcome the problem.

CHAPTER 9

In Which my Life Changed Forever

The pay was slack and the hours were hopeless but I was thrilled to be learning.

I was blessed to be working with two people who were geniuses at what they did: one of the best seminar presenters in the world, and the best copywriter in the country. I listened to them intently, beginning to understand the power of the strategies they were teaching me. I devoured everything they had — books, manuals, tapes, videos.

Work wasn't about money for me, it was about learning.

I worked in a tiny little office next to one of these owners, who constantly hacked at my work until it was perfect.

My natural talent was being developed into a skill through knowledge and working with a master. To truly develop a skill you must work with someone who is so good they can be described as a genius. To work with genius you must sacrifice something, but in my case it was worth it.

I had realised, and my wealthy friend had reinforced to me, that selling was one of the greatest skills a person can have. Not only are salespeople the highest-paid individuals in any company, it is a skill vital to success.

Everybody is a salesperson — even you, whether you know it or not. Every time you ask somebody to do something for you, you are selling; every time you negotiate or come to a deal, you are selling; every time you get your boss to agree to a project or an idea, you are selling. You are selling on a date, selling when you get your children to tidy their room. Everybody can do it and yet few people master it.

"It's too easy for people to think they are not salespeople and yet too hard not to be one," my wealthy friend would say. "All you need is something you believe in and persistence, and you will be a successful salesperson."

And marketing was just "salesmanship in print".

Projects started to pour in and I handled them with ease, each time getting better and better. I was on a roll, and then something happened that would change my life forever: my boss asked me if I thought that I could teach what I was doing to somebody else.

It seemed simple enough. After all, I had learnt sales, marketing, customer service and consulting from scratch. I'd learnt by reading, listening to tapes, attending seminars run by our company, and paying attention when my boss corrected my work. If I could teach myself, surely I could teach others.

My boss told me he had a vision for the company: that young consultants would be able to consult to businesses and improve their profits through the application of a simple system. All we had to do was apply a few basic principles to each business and the profits would start rolling in ... for them and us. I was inspired, but first I had to do it myself.

One of the principles that my boss had taught me is that you always start a sale by discovering the needs of the client. "Ask questions, and then shut up," he would say.

The phone rang and I picked it up. I decided that this caller, whoever it was, would be my first sale.

His name was Phillip, and he had a business problem.

"I'm sure we can help you," I said. "Can you tell me what the problem is?"

Within seconds, Phillip was telling me all about his business and I was taking notes on all the ways I could think of that I could improve it. Once he had outlined his business problem, I told him my ideas and asked him if he would like to be a client.

He asked me how much.

My boss and I hadn't got that far in the conversation, and so I pulled a figure out of the air. "One thousand dollars," I said, thinking that was a lot of money for just some words.

He immediately said, "OK."

That was too quick I thought, and so I added, "A month. That's $1,000 a month."

"Fine," he said, and I had my first client.

It was to be surprising how much impact Phillip would have on my life.

By the end of the day I had three clients. No marketing, no advertising, just listening to people who called in, asking questions and suggesting ways they could improve.

My boss was impressed.

"You're already earning twice as much as we pay you a month — good work — keep this up and we'll have to give you a pay rise."

I took him at his word and started answering all the phone calls that came into the office. I even sold somebody who had the wrong number!

It was easy.

Our business had an excellent reputation with its clients, and the ideas that I had, with the assistance of my boss, were excellent. Soon I was sitting with clients, taking briefs and designing ads and creating strategies for businesses that massively increased their sales.

The funny thing is that all I was teaching them was what I had learnt behind the cash register at the supermarket — smiling and buying. Sales, marketing and customer service.

It was time for our first addition to the team. This person sat with me, listened to what I did and then got clients of their own. Even though they'd never owned a business before in their life, they seemed to be successful. We recruited some more. They seemed to be successful as well.

Soon I was far too busy, handling my own clients and training new people, to sit in on their consultations. But I was sure they'd be just like me — determined to succeed and do anything they could to do so.

I worked hard. I sold new clients during the day, diligently calling people on our database to discover ways we could help. I trained new team members and did my consultations. I rarely had time to prepare for my consultations, but I had been trained so well that I could usually walk in and pull a rabbit out of the hat — "winging it" we called it — and the clients always walked away happy.

I became a "legend" amongst the team and they strived to emulate my success.

I worked well into the night, creating the ads and brochures and sales pieces my clients needed to grow their business and supervising the business plans my team had created.

One of my bosses presented seminars to teach business owners how to improve profits, and so it was natural they would then want support implementing the strategies. From time to time I was allowed to present at the seminars and I loved it. My boss, who was, and still is, one of the best presenters in the world, suggested I had a natural talent and maybe one day I could do it as well as he did.

I remembered as a teenager how much I loved being involved in theatre, and the thrill of presenting for me was to see people come alive with ideas and knowledge that they knew would change their life. Some people find speaking to audiences terrifying, yet I enjoyed it. I was soon to learn mass communication is one of the greatest skills anybody can have, particularly if you love it.

We were so confident of success, we guaranteed our results: we increase your profits or you don't pay. With such a strong guarantee in place, we bumped up our fees. Up they went, and up and up, until we were one of the most expensive consulting companies in the country.

My boss told me and my team to be proud of what we charged. We were after all legends, and as long as we kept getting results for our clients they'd be happy to pay!

Everybody was on commissions and so were highly motivated to get in new clients. And roll in they did. In 12 months the company multiplied its turnover by eight times!

My boss was pleased indeed. He was working less and earning significantly more.

In fact I was the only one who seemed to be working hard. And I was working my butt off.

Lesson

Selling is one of the greatest money-earning skills anybody can have. Everyone is capable of selling.

All you need is something you believe in and persistence, and you will be a successful salesperson!

CHAPTER 10

The First Secret of Money Magnetism

One day, my wealthy friend came to show me his brand-new Ferrari. For once I was not interested in his beautiful toy, its gleaming red paintwork not holding its usual magic.

"What's up?" he asked.

Something had been troubling me for a while now. As I had mastered the art of marketing and applied that knowledge, my income had grown with it. I knew that I was still being positive and working hard, and so I was getting back what I was putting out, but something seemed to be missing.

I asked him why some people seemed to earn so much more than others and yet they didn't seem to work any harder.

"I was waiting for this question," he said. "Have you ever noticed how money sticks like a magnet to some people?"

I had certainly noticed how it had stuck to him. Everywhere he went, everything he did, and everything he owned glimmered with money. Every business deal he undertook seemed to turn to gold, and people were always offering him amazing opportunities.

"I'll be happy to explain the Three Secrets of Money Magnetism, but first let's take a drive," he said, as he fired up the Ferrari.

I had fallen in love with these beautiful cars many years ago. If you see a motor car just as a way of getting from "A" to "B", you will never understand the passion that I feel for these cars. But nobody can fail to see the magnificent craftsmanship and loving attention to detail that has gone into making these fine machines when they get up close to one.

As my wealthy friend pushed the car faster and faster, snapping skilfully through the gears, I gradually forgot my troubled mind and just enjoyed the experience. With the top down, the wind was in my hair, the sun was on my face, my ears were full of the most magnificent sound to be produced by a machine and life was good.

One thing that has always stayed with me from that day is the smell of that car. It is well known that Ferraris drive like no other car, sound like no other car and look like no other car, but few people know that they also smell like no other car.

Finally after pushing the car faster than he should up a winding mountain road, we came to a stop at a lookout where we could see the whole city below us.

"Take a look down there," he commanded, "and tell me what you see."

"A city?" I hesitantly replied, not truly understanding what he was getting at.

"Absolutely," he said. "But look at the houses, the streets, the cars scooting about. What do you notice about them?"

"They all look the same."

"Exactly. When we start out, we are created to be like no other. Each of us is unique, unlike any other person on the planet. Nature creates us, close enough so that we are recognisable as humans but different enough so that no two people are exactly alike.

"And what do we do with that uniqueness? We throw it away. Our life becomes about fitting in with other people. Look at your friends. I bet they are similar to you. I bet they live in similar houses, in similar streets. Drive similar cars, have similar professions, and earn similar incomes. Not exactly the same, but close enough. People like people who are similar to themselves.

"And from here, everything looks the same — it all blends. What stands out though?"

"Well," I said, "the skyscrapers, that church, that factory."

"And why do they stand out?" he asked.

"I guess, because they are different to everything around them."

"Exactly — they are unique. Look at this car. Ferraris are one of the most expensive cars in the world — 10 or 20 times the price of the average car. Are they 10 or 20 times better? No. They are certainly superb, but not that good. Are they 10 or 20 times faster? No. They certainly move quickly, but they are not that fast. So why are they so expensive?"

Now I was catching on. "Because they are unique."

"One of these days we'll make a millionaire out of you!"

He paused for a moment to remove from the windscreen of his beautiful car a bug that had been a king in a former life.

"So," I began, "what you're saying is that things are expensive because they are unique. I guess that means that in order for a person to be 'expensive' they need to be unique as well?"

"Of course. You are paid in direct proportion to your uniqueness. The more people who can do what you do, the less you will be paid. The less people who can do what you do, the more you will be paid. Do you remember when you were working at the supermarket?"

"How could I forget!"

"How many people do you think could do that job?"

"Just about anybody, I guess."

"And how much did you get paid?"

"Sweet Fanny Adams!"

"Now, what happened when you started adding uniqueness into your job — the smiling and buying?"

"I got promoted!"

"Yes — so your uniqueness brought you new opportunities and an increased income."

"And what happened when you changed your standard application letter to something unique?"

"I got the job."

"And now?"

"Well, I guess there aren't too many people who can do what I do. Business owners all want to increase their profits, and I can help them do that. That's pretty unique, and the better I get at it the more money comes in. So what you're saying is that people will pay for uniqueness?"

"Yes. The art to a massive income is to ensure that you understand the three steps to uniqueness: have something that people want, that they are prepared to pay for and that you are the only person who has it.

"And it's no good just having one or two of the three steps. If you have something that people want and are prepared to pay for, but they can get it from a lot of people, than you have too much competition and your uniqueness disappears. If you have something that people want, and you are the only person who has it but they are not prepared to pay, than again you will get nowhere. But if you find a talent, a skill, a product that is genuinely unique, something that people want, will pay for and can only get from you, then you are writing a ticket for riches. Uniqueness is the first Secret of Money Magnetism"

I was catching on now. I often thought it was unfair that I got paid so much more than the receptionist who worked for us. She was wonderful — friendly, helpful, smiling, and made a damn good fresh orange juice, which she lovingly placed on my desk each morning. She seemed to work just as hard as me, and yet I received five times her salary. But now I realised, as nice as she was, there were a lot of people who could do her job. In fact, when the position was advertised, the company had received over 200 applications. Sure, she was unique enough to stand out from those 200 people to get the job, but what she did was not unique enough to warrant the company paying any more for it.

I was starting to understand that it wasn't about whether you were a nice person or a good person, or whether you worked hard or not, it had everything to do with how many people could do what you did.

"The amazing thing," said my wealthy friend, "is that we all start out completely unique. And yet, by the time we get to school, most of has have learnt that in order to 'fit in' and make friends we have to give up most of our uniqueness. Adults scoff at teenagers for being 'different' while still conforming to the 'rules' set by their peers, and yet they don't see that they themselves are doing exactly the same things every day at work.

"Take peak-hour traffic, for example. We are all so conformist that we have to turn up at work at exactly the same time. How stupid is that? So we spend our mornings and afternoons struggling and getting cranky, fighting with all the other conformists to get to one tiny speck on the map all at the same time. No wonder people have such a bad time at work. What they give out they get back. And so we learn to give up our uniqueness to fit in, and so we become like everybody else and at the same time give up our ability to command a large income.

"Take a look at these bugs," he said, as he scraped yet another lifeless shell off his windshield. "They all gave up their lives to an obstacle they couldn't see. If people give up their uniqueness completely, and so many do, they give up their lives to the soulless task of fitting in."

"So, uniqueness pays," I said.

"Yes, but not just any uniqueness mind you. Some people who are 'unique' are just nut cases. And this is where the Second Secret of Money Magnetism comes in. But first, let's have a coffee."

Lesson

The First Secret of Money Magnetism — Uniqueness.

You are paid in direct proportion to your uniqueness. The more people who can do what you do, the less you will be paid. The less people who can do what you do, the more you wil be paid.

If you find a talent, a skill, a product that is genuinely unique, something that people want, will pay for and can only get from you, then you are writing a ticket for riches.

CHAPTER 11

The Second Secret of Money Magnetism

My wealthy friend certainly knew how to live.

We pulled up outside the most expensive coffee house in the city. Amazingly, just as we arrived a car pulled out of a parking space right in front of the café.

"Wow," I said in genuine awe, "I can never get a car park here."

"That's funny," my wealthy friend replied, "I never have any trouble at all."

I was beginning to realise that life was easy for him in more ways than having a lot of money.

I knew about this café, but had never been there. Firstly, because it was so expensive; and secondly, even if I could afford the price of a coffee here, I could never get in because it was so popular.

The café's interior was truly magnificent. Its walls and fittings were made of hand-carved wood, with polished brass and gold filigree detailing. Elaborate, gold-framed original oil paintings were hung on the walls; the furnishing fabrics were of rich silk, wool and cotton; and the waiters were all perfectly dressed with crisp, white, floor-length aprons.

I went to stand in the queue for a table but my wealthy friend signalled for me to follow him. As soon as he was inside, the chief waiter welcomed him like a long lost friend with the Italian greeting, "Ciao."

We were immediately shown to a table which seemed to materialise out of nowhere. My wealthy friend ordered a latte and I ordered an iced chocolate. I suddenly became nervous as I looked at the prices. I know I was earning good money now but I still had debts to pay. Sensing my discomfort, my wealthy friend said, "This one's on me, but watch as he makes our drinks."

A waiter moved at the speed of the Ferrari we had just so recently left. Coffee beans, milk and froth seemed to float through the air and arrive in the cup in a manner that left me breathless. My iced chocolate came together with the syrup swirled in elaborate patterns around the glass and the chocolate in the form of a teddy bear on the top, finished with a flourish of the hand and a thick paper napkin tied around the glass.

And the taste! Magnifique! I couldn't quite place an unusual ingredient — honey maybe?

"Unique, isn't it?" my wealthy friend asked, tearing my thoughts away from the delicious drink before me.

I started to realise why people queued up to spend so much for a "simple" cup of coffee.

A waiter flashed past and left a crystal plate with some biscotti artfully arranged upon it.

"Excuse me," I said, loud enough to stop the waiter in his tracks.

"Yes, sir?"

"I sorry, but we didn't order these."

"I know, sir," he said, and scurried off to another table.

"They're all part of the experience," my wealthy friend said, "they're free!"

I was about to comment, when we were interrupted by the waiter who had greeted us when we first came in. He and my wealthy friend started an animated conversation about his new Ferrari. The man turned out to be much more than chief waiter. He was in fact the owner of the café and owned not one, but three Ferraris. All of a sudden it became apparent just how much money there was to be had from being 'unique'.

Soon the conversation ended and the owner and my wealthy friend exchanged farewell pleasantries.

"Why do you think people come here?" my wealthy friend asked, getting us back on track.

"Because of how unique it is."

"Yes, but it's more than just uniqueness, look around at the people. Do they seem to be enjoying themselves to you?"

I hadn't noticed before how happy people seemed here. Some were chatting, others were talking animatedly, and a few were holding hands in quiet contemplation of their love. There were all different types of people, but they were all taking in and enjoying the ambience of the café.

"The reason people come here is because the experience *adds value* into their lives."

I had never heard that term before. "What do you mean it 'adds value'?"

"Everybody wants the same things in life — the things that have real value. Everybody wants to be healthy, wealthy and happy, and everybody wants love in their life. And we all want extra time to be able to experience these things.

"Look around you. People are here with friends, partners, family and lovers. They are enjoying eating good food and drink served with care and attention. They are being fussed over by the waiter and made to feel special by the owner. Time seems to stand still. Nobody here is hurried, and many an afternoon disappears in laughter. So, not only is it unique, this business is adding value into people's lives. And you will see that people are prepared to pay for it."

I could certainly see that, and I was glad that my wealthy friend was picking up the bill.

I could also see that even though we had been here for over an hour, the queue to get in had not gone down — in fact, if anything, it had got longer. Some people had left and gone elsewhere, but most had persisted in waiting, expressing delight when a waiter eventually showed them to a table.

And nobody had complained about the bill when it arrived, in fact most people were leaving big tips. No wonder the owner had three Ferraris!

"You will find, Peter, that your monetary and intrinsic rewards in life will be in direct proportion to the amount of value that you add into people's lives. When you find ways to add wealth, health, happiness, love or time into people's lives you will be rewarded for that. And remember, what you put out you get back. So the more value you add, the more you will be rewarded."

"OK," I said, "so that's why I'm doing so well at work. I'm helping people make their businesses more profitable through marketing. That's adding Wealth Value, isn't it?" I asked.

"Exactly," my wealthy friend said. "And from what you told me about your work, you're also adding Time Value by teaching business people to systemise their business so they don't have to be there all the time."

Now I was catching on. Uniqueness was fabulous, but by itself was no good – if what you did also added value into people's lives, then you were on to a winner.

All of a sudden I could see why my pay packet had gone up so much. The business I worked for was certainly providing a unique service. We were showing small to medium-sized businesses how to increase their profits through marketing and make best use of their time through systems. This in turn allowed the business owners to spend time away from their businesses, to do things they enjoyed with people they loved, so we were also adding Happiness Value and Love Value into their lives.

When I first looked at the fees the business was charging, I was amazed at how high they were. Now I understood why people were willing to pay so much.

As it was obvious to my wealthy friend that the power of what he was saying was now dawning on me, he seemed very happy with himself.

"Now you seem to be getting it," he said, proud of his student. "When you develop a product or service or skill or tool that is unique, in that it is something people want, that they are prepared to pay for, and that they can only get from you, and it is something that adds more wealth, health, happiness, love or time into people's lives, you will be rewarded in direct proportion to that uniqueness and value. The more you put out — the more value you add — the more you will get back — the more money you will earn.

"When you discover and work these secrets, money starts coming in from all angles. You start to attract it like you are a money magnet. That's why they are called the 'Secrets of Money Magnetism'."

"Yes, I understand that," I said, "and I know why I am getting paid so well, but I seem to have reached a plateau."

"What do you mean?" my wealthy friend asked.

"Well, my pay has gone up dramatically, and I am happy with the value that I am adding, but I am working as many hours as I can and I am working really hard. My boss isn't working any harder and he is benefiting from my work even more than me. How can I keep earning more?"

"Ahh, you're ready for the Third Secret of Money Magnetism. But not now, I have a massage to get to. See if you can figure it out. I'll call you when I have an opportunity to demonstrate it to you."

I went back to work, enthusiastic and looking for ways to add even more value into the lives of the business people I dealt with. I discussed staff training with them and promotional initiatives that might bring more business to them and, as the profits rolled in for them, they referred more and more clients to the business I worked for and the profits rolled in for my boss.

But still it was well after 11.00 p.m. that I would get home, and my beautiful friend started thinking I was having an affair. Arguments started at home and I realised, even though I was adding more wealth, happiness, love and time into the lives of my clients, I was certainly only doing a good job of adding wealth to mine and seemed to be ignoring the other important things in my life.

And I was getting tired.

I loved my work, and I loved the income that came with it, but the fatigue meant I started making the odd mistake, which meant I had to work even longer hours to fix it.

I needed that Third Secret of Money Magnetism!

And yet it took forever for my wealthy friend to call me again for another meeting.

Lesson

The Second Secret of Money Magnetism — Add Value.

When you find ways to add wealth, health, happiness, love or time into people's lives, you will be rewarded for that.

Chapter 12

The Third Secret of Money Magnetism

It was late in the evening when he called, and I had suffered a long day.

"Are you ready for the Third Secret of Money Magnetism?" he asked, bright and cheery as ever.

"About five weeks ago," was my sarcastic reply.

"Well, sorry it's taken so long, but I've been waiting to show you something. Meet me at the construction site tomorrow at 6.00 a.m."

Great, I thought, as I hung up. I've put in a 20-hour day and now he wants me to get up at the crack of dawn for my next lesson!

As I turned up at his construction site, a giant crane was lifting huge concrete slabs. I was handed a bright orange helmet and ear muffs by a worker on the site. The noise was quite loud and it was impossible to hold a conversation with and without the earmuffs, so I stood and watched the work go on as my wealthy friend reviewed plans and schedules with the site foreman.

It became obvious that the concrete slabs being put into place by the crane had been pre-fabricated off site. Workers scurried around guiding the slabs, but the crane was certainly doing the vast majority of the work, and the building was quickly taking shape. In a few hours all the slabs were in place, and the crane had started lifting huge steel girders and frames. These would form the supports for the roof. By noon, the crane had done its work and was ready to be shut down.

I took off my earmuffs.

"Would you like some lunch?" said my wealthy friend.

"Yes, I'm starving!"

"Let me introduce you to a gourmet delight — your shout."

Well, I figured, it wasn't like I couldn't afford one or two extravagances these days.

My wealthy friend led me down to the back of the construction site, over planks spanning trenches, and through half-completed walls, to a back street where the workers from the site had gathered around a truck that seemed to be a mobile café.

"Welcome to the pie cart," said the foreman. "What would you like?"

I checked out the menu and noticed I could have anything I wanted as long as it was wrapped in pastry! I looked around and noticed all the tradespeople were eating meat pies smothered in tomato sauce and drinking coffee-flavoured milk. I thought it was a strange combination. (Since that day I have been on many, many building sites and one thing never changes — the tradespeople always eat meat pies smothered in tomato sauce and drink coffee-flavoured milk.)

My wealthy friend ordered the same combination; however, I couldn't personally stomach it, and so ordered my pie with a soft drink. We sat down with the workers on some large tin cans and ate lunch.

"Simon," my wealthy friend began, directing his question to the foreman, "how much weight could that crane lift?"

"300 tonnes," was Simon's reply.

"How many men would it take to lift that much weight?"

"Well, I'd be guessing but a strong man can lift 100 kilograms, so that means 3000 men."

"And how long would it take to build the same structure we just saw go up in a morning if we were using concrete blocks laid by hand?"

"I'd say it would take 20 men about six or seven working weeks."

"And the cost of that?"

He pulled out his builder's pencil and used a piece of scrap timber as a note pad. "Well, let's see, at $40 per hour per man that would work out at about $200,000 in labour costs."

"And how much did today cost me?"

All of a sudden the foreman got a bit suspicious of all the questions and asked, "Why, are you looking for a discount or something?"

"No," laughed my wealthy friend, "I'm just about to make a point to my young friend here."

"OK, the offsite labour was about $30,000, and transport here came to about $20,000, the crane hire was $10,000 and the operator was $500. We had 10 men for six hours at $40 per hour and two at $100, plus the site inspection and health inspectors. I'd say it added up to about $65,000."

"So, by using the crane I saved myself $135,000."

"I guess you did," said the foreman, nodding in agreement.

"So what do you think, Peter?"

"Pretty impressive," I said. "You've saved a lot of money, but how does this apply to me?"

"In a number of ways...Money saved is money made. If I had used the old methods of construction, I would have had to pay out $135,000 in additional costs. That money can now be used by me for other projects. So I have created wealth by using leverage.

"Imagine what it would have cost and how long it would have taken if we had to use those 3000 men? The Egyptians understood the concept of leverage and they used it to build the pyramids, rolling huge blocks of stone on wood and then lifting them by cranes and levers into positions so perfectly fitted you can't get a butter knife between them.

"And today I showed you how leverage can be applied to build a warehouse in one morning when normally it would have taken six weeks. So not only did it cost me much less to build, it means the property can be making me money earlier. Those six weeks of rent will be about $30,000.

"Leverage can be applied in many ways. Today you have seen mechanical leverage used to save time and money. Leverage can also be systems that allow you to work more efficiently. Leverage can be understanding how to delegate. It can also be in employing staff, or using mass communication. What you do — marketing — is leverage. It sends a selling message to more than one person at once.

"You can also use financial leverage; for example, borrowing money to buy property or shares. And you can use leverage to influence people by discovering what motivates them and talking in terms and language that appeals to them. When you apply leverage to a good product or service, it increases the returns and rewards that you get.

"So, for example, let's say that you can find a way to systemise what you do in your consulting. That would enable you to teach somebody else to do it. Or if there were repetitive things in what you do, you could systemise those and give them to somebody else. Alternatively if there is some particular skill that you are good at but your work requires you to do something that you are not so good at, then you could get somebody who is better suited to that work to do it so you can concentrate on what you are good at. In this way, leverage would enable you to serve more clients in the same time and therefore earn a higher income.

"Think, Peter — are there general strategies that you teach to every business person you speak to? You could put those strategies into a briefing paper and send it to all your clients before your consultations. This would be using leverage to save you time explaining the concepts, freeing you up to serve more clients. Or you could write and sell books or deliver seminars as a separate way to generate income.

"Any way that you can impact or sell to more than one person at a time, make or distribute things, or do something once that can be duplicated over and over again, that's leverage. Factories and manufacturing, assembly lines and workshops are all leverage, enabling a company to mass produce items cheaper and faster.

"If you are successful at making something and you find a way to make it faster, quicker, or cheaper, then that's leverage. If you are successful at selling one thing and you can find a way to sell it to more than one person at a time, then that's leverage. If you can find a way of doing something over and over again without you having to be there, then that's leverage. It magnifies your results because instead of you doing it one at a time you can do it with dozens, perhaps hundreds or thousand of people at once.

"Leverage is the most exciting of the Three Secrets of Money Magnetism because it magnifies your results. But be careful, because leverage can also magnify problems, mistakes and losses. If you apply leverage to something that loses money, it will compound your losses as well."

"I see," I said. "So leverage is all about doing more with what you have?"

"Exactly. The wealthy are always looking for ways to apply leverage. They do it in their marketing, they do it in their manufacturing and in their hiring, and they do it in their negotiations. If you understand what makes somebody tick, what motivates them, what their soft spot is, you have leverage over them. I know it sounds mercenary, but it's true.

"Leverage is the greatest amplifier of money. If you have uniqueness, can add value and then apply leverage, you will certainly have money attracted to you as if you were a magnet."

"I get it," I said. "So when my boss employed me and taught me how to consult, he was applying leverage."

"Spot on."

"And when I systemised what I did so I could do it over and over again without thinking, I was applying leverage. And when we employed other people to do what I did, we were applying leverage. And every mail-out we do to our clients is applying mass-communication leverage. And when we guarantee our results, we are applying emotional leverage on our clients because they all want to be sure they are going to get value for money."

"Yes," my wealthy friend said. "It seems your boss is very good at applying leverage."

He sure is, I thought. I had seen the results myself. Money was pouring in.

"I just hope," said my wealthy friend as he walked me off the construction site, "that your system is robust enough to cope with so much leverage applied."

"What do you mean?" I asked, confused.

"Every crane has a load-bearing limit," he replied cryptically.

I walked to my car, past the workers packing up the massive crane, and left with a slightly ominous feeling about that last comment.

Lesson

The Third Secret of Money Magnetism — Leverage.

When you apply leverage to a good product or service, it increases the returns and rewards that you get. But if you apply leverage to something that loses money, it will compound your losses.

CHAPTER 13

Where our Vision Outran my Skills

Something strange was going on, that was for sure. I just couldn't tell what it was, at first.

My team was happy — they "lucked into" a job where they needed no skills, followed a template and earned a small fortune. My clients were happy — we increased their profits or they didn't pay. And I was earning what seemed to be a small fortune.

But I sensed that something was wrong. We seemed to be cutting corners. I was way too busy to be attending to my clients properly, and some of my team had even more clients than me — how could they possibly be looking after everybody properly?

Our company was expanding rapidly but now I was way too busy to keep up learning.

Soon my management skills were pushed to the limit.

I had trouble communicating with my team of consultants. Our team-motivation sessions had turned into self-congratulatory exercises regardless of whether it was justified or not. From being proud of "knowing my stuff" so well that I didn't need to do preparation before my consultations, now everybody seemed to be "winging it" and I wasn't sure they were getting the same results as me.

All the reports from the consulting team were that our clients were happy. Every month the team members filled in reports stating the number of consultations they had with their clients and claimed their commissions based on their servicing of the clients. There didn't seem to be any problem there.

I monitored the refunds from our guarantee and there were only a couple, so nothing seemed out of order there.

Sales were still sky rocketing. We were adding more and more clients and more and more team members to service them. Training of new members was getting a bit slack — we were all too busy, but none of our clients seemed to be complaining, well at least not to me.

So, sales were coming, the team seemed to be doing their job, very few refunds were being paid out, and yet the bank account was not going up. In fact, in a few alarming months, it was going down. Now my boss was worried, and so was I. No matter where I looked, though, I couldn't find any problems, so we called in the accountants. It took them about five months to unravel the mystery.

By this time, the company was bleeding. Sales had slowed dramatically and now more money was flowing out each month than was flowing in. Once the accountants pointed out what was happening, it seemed obvious. I was kicking myself that I hadn't seen it.

Our commissions were based on the amount of time that our consultants spent with the client, not on the amount of money they collected.

Our consultants had run out of ideas long before the clients had perceived they had got value from the astronomical fees.

Because we never thought to match up their commission claims with the clients actually paying, we didn't notice that most of them had stopped paying some time ago.

You see, we thought that clients asking for refunds would tell us when things were wrong, but the consultants figured out that as long as they kept the client "on board" — regardless of whether they paid or not — they might just be able to pull a rabbit out of the hat and the client wouldn't ask for a refund of their fees. Most of the time no rabbit came, and so our consultants kept working for free, sometimes for month after month, afraid to ask for payment in case that triggered a refund and we discovered just how far behind they were. At the same time, they kept claiming their commission based on their servicing of the client. Costs mounted up. It cost so much to service the clients that — rather than consulting with them for free for three months — we would have been better off just issuing the refund, as it would have cost us less.

Our clients had heard the rumours that the systems weren't working and had stopped buying. In fact many were now openly questioning that we had ever had a success. I knew we had, but now I didn't know what to do.

My boss looked to me to fix the problem, my team looked to me for help, and our clients looked to me for explanations.

The vision had outgrown my skills.

I was lost, stressed and had no idea what to do. In desperation, I asked my wealthy friend for advice.

"Some ideas are just too flawed to work. Nothing will fix them. You'll remember that I told you it was dangerous to apply such strong leverage to an idea that was fundamentally flawed. Leverage in that circumstance will only make the end come quicker. Remember — leverage magnifies problems as well as successes."

"But what should I do?" I asked.

My wealthy friend said simply, "They shoot sick horses."

And so I was alone.

My once-fabulous team were in revolt, and were either resigning or being fired as we cut back expenses.

There was only one thing for me to do — I resigned. Remarkably, my bosses refused and wanted me to stay on in an effort to pull things together.

There was certainly no doubt that I was still getting results with my clients and there was certainly no doubt that I was able to "rescue" a number of my former team's clients, but it wasn't enough.

My two bosses kept giving me conflicting instructions.

Soon nobody knew what was going on and, just three months after refusing my resignation, my boss fired me. At least he did it himself — most people only got letters.

Some months later it became obvious why I had received so many conflicting instructions from my two bosses — their once mighty partnership was on the rocks and they had decided to split up the business.

One of my bosses went on to be a worldwide and highly successful seminar presenter. His business was highly successful and after a decade he sold it for millions. I lost touch with my other boss.

In the hands of experienced people who were well trained, the ideas and concepts we had been working with could easily have been translated into a successful consulting practice. In the early days, when our people were highly trained, motivated and well supervised, the results for our clients were fabulous. My wealthy friend later explained that many a great idea had been dashed on the rocks of poor implementation.

And yet, I am forever grateful to both of my bosses for giving me the greatest business education on the face of the planet. For many years I thought about that business, what we'd done right, what we'd done wrong.

Lesson

Skills need to be constantly improved in order for you to be able to carry out your vision.

CHAPTER 14

In Which Life Turns Back to Bliss

Armed with my payout from my previous job and some savings I had managed to gather, I went out on my own, hung out my shingle and set up shop as a business consultant.

The two things I enjoyed doing most were writing advertising copy and presenting, so I decided I would have a small advertising agency where I would get my clients by presenting seminars. I also wanted to explore one aspect of leverage that particularly fascinated me — the concept of franchising.

I figured that seeing as I earned only a fraction of the amount the company had billed for my work in commission, I could afford to charge considerably less than my previous employer did for my skills, and I could work less and earn more.

I was in no hurry to get clients though. I was exhausted from working so hard at my previous job and drained from the emotion of seeing a vision I had worked so hard to build and believed in fall apart.

I never personally approached any of the clients of my former employer. They just sought me out. My very first client, Phillip, was the first to find me. He rang me to ask what I was doing. When I explained that I had set up on my own, he asked if I wanted him as a client. So it was ironic that my first-ever client became the first client of my fledgling business.

More clients sought me out and soon my little business was booming. It proved that the idea my former boss had was right, and that the concepts we were teaching were good — they just needed to be applied in a different manner.

Soon I was earning more than enough to change our lifestyle. My beautiful friend and I moved to a seaside cottage, with a loft bedroom, a fireplace, our own private beach and views out over the bay that went on forever.

I rarely got out of bed before 11.00 a.m., worked for about three hours a day in my office in the cottage's boatshed, and spent the rest of my time with my beautiful friend.

We applied the principles of Money Magnetism, creating uniqueness through refining our marketing systems and processes so they almost always worked (a huge feat, as there is a well-known saying about marketing attributed to various famous business people: "50% of the money I spend on advertising works — I just wish I knew which 50%"), value adding by getting to know our clients' businesses intimately and really improving their profits, decreasing the time they spent in their business and increasing their quality of life.

We spent hours on our private beach, reading and lying in the sun, improving our knowledge and our tans at the same time. We bought our first expensive car, a brand-new BMW. Life was as blissful as it was profitable. In my first year out I was to earn three times what I had working for my previous employers and worked about a quarter of the hours.

My beautiful friend was determined to "learn the business". At first I was reluctant, given my experience at my former work — where inexperienced people were let loose on the clients – but she convinced me to give her a go. With her determination to prove herself, she soon became as good a consultant as me (some say better!).

I soon saw the distinction between what I and my beautiful friend had done and what the people employed at my former work had done. Both of us immersed ourselves in learning, because knowledge had become a quest. And we had another Key to Success — what my wealthy friend called "personal buy in". In other words, we both had something to prove, whereas the people employed at my former work were only given the most basic of training and were told they were legends long before they had proved themselves.

Our income doubled in just a few months.

My beautiful friend suggested that I run my first seminar. I researched it for seven months, immersing myself in the knowledge so it became second nature to me. Then Phillip convinced a colleague of his to talk about me at an industry event, and soon I had 200 business cards shoved into my hands.

We charged as much as we dared for the seminar — about half as much as we had charged in my previous work, but still three or four times more than "ordinary" presenters charged. My wealthy friend convinced me the fee was fine — "This idea had 'legs'," he said. After all, I had done the research, tested and double tested the strategies, had ample evidence they would work in real businesses using my test-case consulting clients, and I was adding heaps of value into my clients' businesses and lives.

I carefully prepared the marketing, using all the techniques I had learnt.

We used the 200 business cards as the basis for our address list, and as we gingerly handpacked all the envelopes we wished each envelope luck in its quest to find us business. I couldn't face selling myself, so we put our pager number on the letter and asked for mail responses only.

And respond they did. A total of 21 people booked in, which was more than a 10% response rate (awesome when you consider that most direct mail gets less than 1% response).

My beautiful friend and her mother acted as support staff, and we took ourselves ever so seriously.

I was so determined to give my clients value for money during the four-day seminar that we stayed there until 11.00 p.m. on the first night, after midnight on the second night, 1.00 a.m. on the third night and we finished at 2.00 a.m. on the last night. I was exhausted, and so were my clients, but the seminar was a resounding success with my delegates going back to the industry and raving.

During the seminar, one of the delegates asked me my idea of the perfect business. In the next hour I laid out in detail exactly how I would design, set up, run and market a model business in their industry. They were fascinated. Nobody had ever put that much thought into it before — especially an "outsider". I explained to them that I had spent seven months in designing the four-day seminar, and challenged them to imagine what it would have been like if they had spent seven months designing their business before starting it. I told this little group that I thought I could franchise this idea and make it a success.

Phillip had an idea — if I wanted to build a franchise, he would be willing to be my first franchisee.

We were on our way!

Lesson

When you are on track and enjoying yourself, things will happen easily.

CHAPTER 15

In Which I Fight With a Boat

"Coming about," my wealthy friend yelled.

I ducked to avoid being swept off this magnificent yacht by the huge boom travelling over my head at a frightening speed, and then began winching frantically to pull in the sheet and avoid the fury of the skipper for not doing a good enough job.

I understood why my wealthy friend loved skippering his racing yacht. Apart from the thrill of it, and the precision of drilling a highly dedicated and experienced team working in perfect harmony in pursuit of one goal, being a skipper on a boat was one of the last bastions of pure dictatorship, where the skipper's word was never questioned and when he yelled "Jump", the crew responded with "How high?"

I was amazed at how everything was coming together for me so well since I had been fired from my previous job. I understood that I was harnessing the Key to Wealth, applied knowledge, and the Key to Success, getting back what I was putting out, and applying the Three Secrets of Money Magnetism, but it had never been this "easy" before. I had asked my wealthy friend if he had any observations on all of this.

"Yes, and I call it 'High Level Weirdness'," he said.

Of course I had to have a practical demonstration, and so I found myself in a spray jacket as one of his minion crew in a 300-kilometre ocean race. The first day on board, as my lack of sailing skills showed through, I certainly ran the risk of being keel hauled or hung from the mast, or being forced to walk the plank (not that this 30-metre, glistening fibreglass and chrome thoroughbred racing yacht had such a thing), but as I got to know what was required of me, I settled down and was able to admire how perfectly the crew operated as a team.

Not only were the crew members precise and well coordinated, I realised they had only one task allotted to them and they had mastered it. My job was simply manning one of the seemingly endless winches that tugged on the "sheets" (ropes) that tightened or loosened the sails. I really had only two tasks, winding in and letting out.

I knew that when the skipper yelled "Ready about!" I leapt off my bum and got ready to winch. When he yelled "Coming about!" I simply winched like hell for 20 or so seconds until I could winch no more, and then sat down and waited for my next order.

"This is how inexperienced people learn a task," my wealthy friend barked, "break it down into something simple and drill them in it until they can do it in their sleep."

And do it in our sleep we did.

"Look at this crew," he said. "Yesterday you were all landlubbers, and today you are a highly oiled, precision machine working together in perfect harmony."

He certainly had a point. And we were doing well, being sixth overall in the race and having a good chance at winning on handicap.

"What did you mean earlier, when you referred to High Level Weirdness?" I asked in a break between winching.

"Well," he said, pausing to readjust his jauntily placed skipper's cap for theatrical impact (if he'd had a snow-white beard and pipe, the effect would have been complete), "people who understand what I am about to say consider it quite normal, but people who have never heard of it before think it is weird. And when it is explained thoroughly, it's sometimes considered *highly* weird."

"I see," I said, not really seeing at all.

"Take a look at this yacht. We are pulled along by an invisible force. People think that the wind pushes sailboats, but in fact this is not true. The wind creates a pressure differential between the different sides of the sail; that is, there is more pressure on one side of the sail than the other. But it is a universal law that everything must be in balance and that nature abhors a vacuum and will rush to fill it wherever one is found.

"So, as the wind creates a pressure differential between one side of the sail and the other, nature attempts to correct this imbalance by dragging the air from one side of the sail to the other. The sail provides a physical barrier to this, and so the boat is actually pulled forward by this pressure difference. You can't see this force but you know it is powerful.

"With a bit of leverage assistance through design and engineering, this 100-tonne boat can be pulled forward by the tiniest of breezes."

I couldn't argue with that. Yesterday the breeze had been so slight I couldn't even feel it on my skin, and yet the boat had been quietly cruising at about half its top speed.

"While ever there is wind we can harness it. You will also have observed that our ability to judge precisely the direction and strength of the wind will determine our performance.

"Look up at the sails," he said, "and you will see the boat is in perfect trim — in other words, perfectly in balance with the winds that are pulling it forward and the ocean that is keeping it afloat. Now take a look at the speed we are doing and how effortlessly we are doing it."

I looked around. The boat was gliding through the water at a fast rate and the crew were relaxed in their positions awaiting their next order. The poor folk acting as human ballast were dangling their legs over the side of the boat and gazing out to the horizon with glazed looks on their faces.

And so I agreed with his assessment of our performance. "Everything is in perfect balance."

"Come take the helm."

"Do I get to wear the silly hat?" I asked irreverently.

"Shut up and steer," he barked back. "And if you lose me too much speed, I'll cut out your rations for dinner!"

I gripped the wheel for grim death, every minor movement of the boat forcing an involuntary input from me. I had steered sailing boats many times before but never something as big and complex as this boat. The crew would look up alarmed as the boat slewed and cut around in the water, but quickly resigned themselves to the extra work I had brought on.

"See how much extra work everybody has to do in the hands of an inexperienced skipper?" My wealthy friend was stating the obvious.

"The force of the wind is still there, the boat hasn't changed, only the steerer has changed, and yet look at how perfectly nature copes. The crew have automatically adjusted to your hamfisted style. Every mistake you make is automatically corrected by the crew. And yet it is not your inexperience that is the problem, it is your personal concern about being inexperienced that is the problem. Just relax, let the boat steer herself.

"We'll continue this discussion when you get the hang of it — wake me when you can hold the boat on course using just two fingers on the wheel," he said, as he settled down for a bit of a snooze, his cap pulled down to cover his eyes.

Of course he was right. As I lightened my grip on the wheel and didn't try to correct every little movement and adjustment of the boat, the crew were able to relax again and the boat's performance picked up considerably. I carefully checked the radar and breathed a sigh of relief that all the boats that had been behind us before I had taken the wheel were still behind us. My wealthy friend took his yacht racing (and his golf) very, very seriously!

After a little while my wealthy friend stirred. "Mmm," he murmured. "You seem to be doing well. See how simple it is when you relax and allow everything to happen naturally? Now, let's just get the boat out of trim a bit shall we?"

"John," he ordered one of the crew, "just tighten up that sheet a bit will you? And Peter, keep the boat on the same heading."

I did as I was told and discovered that two fingers was no longer enough. As John pulled in more and more of the sail, I had to apply more and more pressure on the wheel the keep the boat heading in the same direction. It was becoming quite an effort.

The boat heeled over further and further, the human ballast

leaning out further and further in an effort to provide assistance. It became quite difficult to hold on — I had to wedge my feet into the base of the wheel housing. And the boat was complaining too, creaking and groaning, and the chrome fittings were banging on the aluminium mast.

"Now hold it on course, Peter, and watch that the compass doesn't move a bit."

The boat was fighting me and fighting hard as John kept winding in the sail. I heard plates crashing in the galley below and the cook cursing. The crew all watched intently at the task the skipper had set me. I was sure they were taking bets over who would win, John or me.

The awesome power of the sails was getting far too much. I was holding on with all my might, and I swear I could see the keel of the boat out of the water. All my weight was applied to the wheel to keep the boat on course.

One of the other race boats had caught up to us and its crew looked on in bemusement at the titanic (excuse the pun) battle.

Then my leg slipped and I lost my grip on the wheel. The mighty boat sensed its opportunity and with all its force corrected the indignity that had been forced upon it. The wheel spun rapidly and the heavy keel forced the boat back down into the water so quickly I was terrified we might capsize. The sails were crashing around us and the noise was terrible. The crew hung on for dear life — luckily, they were all wearing their mandatory life vests. And suddenly it was all over, and the boat stopped dead in the water, the metal stays clanging as the sailed luffed in the wind.

"Whoa!" my wealthy friend exclaimed. "That was one hell of a ride! OK everybody, let's get her moving again and check for any damage."

Once I had recovered and caught my breath, and the boat was back sailing again, my lesson continued . . .

"Life, like sailing, should never be difficult. Remember when you relaxed and allowed the boat to steer itself? All you needed to do was tell her what direction you wanted to go, trim the sails and pay attention to any changes in the breeze. Steering and progress was effortless. If the wind changed direction slightly, it was simply a matter of subtle adjustments. As long as you were paying attention to the breeze, nothing difficult came along.

"Life is exactly the same. All we have to do is tell life where we want to go, set a direction and pay attention to the breeze. When you do something, you will get subtle feedback on your direction. If you take an action, you will get a positive or negative response. If you relax and become adept at interpreting these subtle signals, your boat of life will always be in trim and you will glide effortlessly from one success to another without stress or strife.

"Even if we encounter a massive storm, we have to trust in our boat. And this boat is strong. We simply turn the boat into the wind and ride out the storm. It's a bit rough for a while but we are safe and ready to continue sailing as soon as the storm dies down.

"You saw as we changed something on the boat, in this case the trim, you had to work harder and harder to stay on course. What happens in life is the breeze often shifts. Instead of adjusting our steering, we often struggle against the breeze and then have to work harder and harder to stay on course. Eventually we are fighting so hard, we forget the direction and focus on the struggle. We fight until we are exhausted but the leverage of the Universe will always win, and we will be brought back to our path just as dramatically as the boat came back to neutral.

"Worse than that, though, is that most people never get as far as we got on the boat. The resistance to their direction builds up, and they turn the wheel just so slightly to keep going forward, but then they are off course and have to struggle again. Their life becomes a constant struggle, and they are always heading just so slightly away from their goal so it becomes unattainable. If this goes on long enough, they start to think that goals are unobtainable in general and then they just resign themselves to the struggle.

"The Universe has to be in balance, so allow struggle to be your guide. When things get difficult, you are either off course — not doing what you are supposed to be doing — or the breeze had changed and you haven't noticed. Get back on course or adjust to the change, and the struggle will disappear."

This got me thinking. Obviously this is what happened at my former job. We had started off on course with a great idea and a good crew. But as we grew, the wind had changed. We tried to stay on course without adjusting anything, until the business "boat" crashed back to balance.

When I established my own new business on the principles of unique knowledge, value and leverage, things had become easy and my business powered along effortlessly at a great rate of knots.

"OK, I understand that," I said, "but it doesn't explain exactly all these coincidences that have been popping up. Like my first client in my old job becoming the first client of my new business, and him bumping into a colleague who talked about me at an industry seminar just as I needed clients for my seminars. And even little things like the exact car that I wanted being discounted by the dealership the day before I went in to drive it. Doesn't that strike you as odd?"

"Ahh, so at last we get to the High Level Weirdness," my wealthy friend observed, as we crossed the finishing line of the race.

His demonstration to me had cost us dearly and we had slipped five places, costing us our handicap win.

It must have been a very important point indeed for my wealthy friend to have given up a win and the chance of adding another trophy to his collection. It amused me that those $20 plastic cups had cost him hundreds of thousands, perhaps even millions, to win.

Lesson

The Universe is always in perfect balance. While you remain on course to your dreams, life will be simple.

When things get difficult, you are either not doing what you are supposed to be doing or you need to adjust your approach.

CHAPTER 16

The Law of Universal Convergence

"Your brain cannot distinguish between a well-formed idea and reality. Dreams can seem real, actors on a screen can fool you into believing you are watching reality, but your brain is more powerful than any movie," said my wealthy friend, in between bites on his lobster as we sat in the gourmet restaurant overlooking the marina where we had just left his yacht to the crew. Just like your brain, nature cannot distinguish between a powerful idea and 'reality' either."

"I can see what you mean by this being High Level Weirdness," I said. "I'm not sure I understand."

"That's OK, it's rare that somebody gets it on their first exposure to the concept. You will remember we discussed how every living and inanimate thing is made of atoms held together by electromagnetic charges. Brain waves create electromagnetic charges as well. These electric waves can be monitored by an electro-encephalograph. In other words, your thoughts are electric pulses of energy, in exactly the same way that an animal or a tree is made up of electric charges. To nature, a well-formed thought is as good as reality. It cannot distinguish between the two.

"When you formulate a quality idea and commit to its transformation into reality, this creates a vacuum. There is a differential created between the imagination and reality. This differential is just as invisible as the pressure differential created by the wind on the sail of a boat, and just as powerful.

"Because the thought does not actually have physical form, nature sets about balancing itself by turning your ideas into concrete reality. It has to — remember, it's just following its own immutable laws.

"If you forget the idea, if your thoughts are fuzzy, unformed, or if you do not commit to your idea, you have automatically balanced the system and nature has to do nothing. Your idea loses its charge and disappears. As long as you continue to have the thoughts and they are clear and well formed, nature will turn your ideas into reality for you. Of course, you have to participate in its creation by keeping the idea well formed and 'supervising' its creation, just as when sailing you have to pay attention to the subtle changes in the breeze, keep the boat well trimmed and steer towards your destination.

"There is a famous story about Walt Disney. It is little known that Disneyland was merely a prototype for his Disney World theme park. He died before the park was completed. The story goes that an interviewer was talking to Roy Disney, Walt's older brother, and had commented on what a shame it was that Walt did not live to see the dream finished. Roy is said to have replied, 'It is because Walt saw his dream finished and real in his head as clearly as if it had been built that it is here today for us to enjoy.'

"Every idea needs resources to bring it into reality. You can either pay for those resources, and this is costly indeed, or you can have nature, the Universe, provide them for you.

"Those coincidences you were talking about are nature's way of creating your ideas. It's called Universal Convergence. In other words, all the power of the Universe converges on your idea and creates the opportunities, resources, people and situations for your ideas to become reality. If you stay alert to the possibilities, you will notice these coincidences and be able to act on them.

"Many people never see their good ideas into reality because they don't notice the resources the Universe is summoning for them. Big ideas take quite some time to manifest, and the Universe has to do considerable work to bring together all the disparate pieces of the puzzle that will become your idea — people, resources, experiences, learnings — all of which are critical for your ideas to work. You may not have the experience or skills necessary to cope with the idea, so the Universe will set about educating you first.

"The Universe is not hampered by time and so it goes about its work as quickly as it can, which is sometimes far too slow for those of us who don't notice the subtle things, the small coincidences, the little doors that are opened, the paths that are made for us to get us in the right direction. When these people give up on their idea, the system is re-balanced and all the work that the Universe has done goes down the drain. This is why great visions sometimes fail.

"Similarly, entrepreneurs who could be great but who are impatient often go far too fast for the people around them. And, because their minds are often so quick, their ideas become well formed quicker than the Universe can create. Instead of having patience and relaxing, like you did when steering the boat, they push things along by adding their own resources. They over borrow or spend so much in bringing their idea into reality that it can never be viable in this world.

"Again they fail, not because they didn't have a great idea, but simply because they did not have the patience to allow things to happen in the natural order. Great things take time to build. More importantly, it takes time for slower minds to come around and for ignorance to be replaced with enlightenment.

"How many great feats of infrastructure do you know of — great companies, buildings, new technology — that is created, often at huge cost, only to fail almost immediately because the cost far exceeded the revenue? And yet how often do you hear of somebody snapping up those things for a song when they are sold off, only to make a success of the idea because their costs were much lower?

"Often the people who thought of the idea are left broke, wondering what went wrong. If they had been patient and allowed the Universe to do its work, bring together all the resources necessary over time, paying attention to the opportunities that are presented and stewarding the idea into reality, they would have not only been able to complete their work, but have been able to take advantage of its success. This is what the saying 'all in good time' is referring to.

"The Law of Universal Convergence can work for you or against you. In exactly the same way as a good idea will be created into reality, something that will inevitably be bad for you can be created too. This is why, when people worry and stress and focus on the negative, bad things can sometimes happen to them. It's not because they are bad people, it's just because of what is being created around them.

"And remember your lesson from the sailing. If you are struggling, it's nature's way of telling you to adjust course. People keep doing the same things over and over again and they expect things to change. The definition of 'frustration' is doing the same thing harder and expecting a different result. And yet that is most people's wealth creation strategy. They figure that if they keep doing what they're doing now, but just work a little bit harder and try a little bit more, they'll get there. They won't. They'll wind up frustrated and exhausted. But if you have patience and stay alert, the Universe will always provide everything you need to carry out your plans."

"OK, so let me see if I've got this," I said, still not 100% sure I was sure. "When you think a thought it is transmitted electrically. The Universe picks up on those thoughts and 'thinks' they are real; but, because they are not real, there is a differential created that the Universe has to 'fix'. It then brings together, over time, all the resources that are necessary to create the idea in a concrete form. All you have to do is be alert for the coincidences and opportunities and be prepared to stay on course and adjust if necessary."

"Exactly, you're catching on quickly these days."

"So all I have to do is think up an idea, and nature will do all the work?" I asked.

"In a fashion. You still have to stay committed to the idea, develop your skills so you can handle it, and coordinate all the resources so that they work together to see the job done. Great minds and highly successful people have known about the power of these Universal Convergences for a long time. Horace Walpole called it 'serendipity' — pleasant coincidence creating great luck and fortune by happenstance.

"The Universe loves providing, so you'll quickly get to enjoy the game of conjuring things out of thin air. Remember, give it a little bit of notice, and make sure you are very clear on what you want and when you want it, and keep the vision firm in your head. When you get good at this you can 'command' the Universe to deliver at will. You might like to start with simple things like car parks."

All of a sudden it became clear to me why my wealthy friend never had any trouble getting car parks. In a High Level Weirdness sort of way, the Universe "created" them for him! And sure enough, I started to get car parks exactly where I wanted them with alarming regularity.

I rang a resort, wishing to book their most popular room at their busiest time of the year just one day before I wanted to stay there. Happily for me, they had just received a cancellation. It was a better room than the one I had requested but they were happy to discount it to the lower rate to make sure it was booked!

I would be running late for an appointment and all the traffic lights would stay green, putting me back on track.

I would need something in my business, and out of the blue I would get a phone call from somebody who could provide it for me.

I was amazed and delighted to play the little game with the Universe at getting the things I wanted, but it was obvious to me that there was an awesome power waiting to be tapped that had big plans for me and my future.

Lesson

Coincidences are nature's way of creating your ideas. Universal Convergence occurs when all the power of the Universe converges on your idea and creates the opportunities, resources, people and situation for your ideas to become reality. If you stay alert to the possibilities, you will notice these coincidences and be able to act on them.

Chapter 17

In Which Tragedy Strikes

My father infuriated me and I totally mystified him. He was old school, straight up and down and by the book, whereas I was always throwing the book away and coming up with a new way. He had never understood me and I didn't understand him.

We had not been talking much since my first business had gone broke. He had reluctantly backed me with all his meagre finances after extracting a begrudging assurance from me that everything was going to be fine, and he had lost everything with it.

Now that I was doing OK, I had offered to pay him back but he had refused. I'm not sure why — stubborn pride or maybe because I had let him down so often before he didn't want to believe me only to be let down again? He was happy that I was doing well, but our relationship was still strained after too many arguments over where the money had gone when the business failed.

He had worked all his life to get the one thing my mother and he were most proud of — a home of their own. And they lost it all in a few months. In fact, it was nothing short of amazing that we were speaking at all, given the circumstances. And so it was highly unusual when he rang to summon me to a family conference. We were not the type of family that had conferences. We were not the type of family that even talked!

I walked into their rented flat and sat down with my mother, father and brother. The mood was sombre.

"I have cancer," my father announced. "It's in my throat. The doctors said it was from my smoking, which I have to give up, but the good news is that I have an 85% chance of beating it and I'm going to take those odds and fight!"

My father was a strong man. If anybody could beat it he could, but I could tell by the wavering in his voice that he wasn't totally convinced.

That was it. End of family meeting.

I decided the best way for me to deal with this news was to follow what I had learnt in the last couple of years. My first "weapon" in the war to save my father would be knowledge. So I started researching the disease and how to beat it. I consulted the doctors and they said that anything I did probably wouldn't help much but, if it made me feel better, it wouldn't bother them if I tried. "Quacks!" I thought, and turned to nature.

I put Dad on a special diet of fruits and vegetables, and high doses of anti-oxidants and cancer-fighting vitamins and herbs. If nothing else, he was eating well, and this would help keep up his strength for his body to fight. This regime seemed to be going well, until one day, some months into his radiology, I had a call from the hospital — my father was "not responding to the treatment".

As I walked through the oncology ward I thought it was a marvel that anybody got out of here alive. It was painted grey and lit coldly with fluorescent light. The doctors and nurses were trying hard, and they seemed to have a soft spot for my dad — after all he was a funny and charming man — but I guess years of being surrounded with death and disease had dulled their senses a bit and you could tell they were detached just to cope.

I walked into my father's room and saw that he was ghostly white. Whereas he normally sat up in bed waiting to pass a sassy remark to one of the nurses, he was slumped down, staring at the window, looking into space.

"What's wrong?" I asked.

"It's not shrinking, the treatment isn't working. Look's like it's got me."

"No it hasn't, Dad," I cried. "You've got to keep fighting. For me, for Mum."

I don't think he was expecting such emotion from me. I crawled up on the bed and hugged him.

"It's just no good," he said, "and I just don't want to be a burden."

All of a sudden his life made sense to me. All our fights, all our disagreements, every time we had clashed, wasn't about him trying to control me, it was his way of trying to help. His whole married life he had been working for his family, to give us what he thought we needed in his own way. In his simple way, he had tried to do what every good parent tries to do — look after his son.

He was looking at me in the same way he always had, an expression on his face that I had always interpreted as disdain, but now I realised it was just quizzical, trying to see if I shared the same feelings of love for him as he had for me.

The fog had cleared, and after 25 years I was able to see what a wonderful man he was. His parenting skills were limited, but he had tried as hard as he could to do the right thing in a funny sort of way; and all of a sudden, instead of "hating" him for his interfering and domineering ways, I loved him for the help, assistance and guidance he had always been there to give.

"Dad, you have looked after us all your life, now it's your turn to be looked after. We'll beat this thing — together."

We held each other tight and I could feel his tears dripping onto my shoulder through the fabric of my shirt, just as my tears dripped on him. We stayed like that for a long time, not wanting to break the moment, until a nurse came in with his dinner. Our outpouring of emotion had helped but I could tell that there was a different sense about him, one that I hadn't experienced before, and I realised he was making his peace, finishing things up and putting things right. But that wasn't good enough for me. Now that I had experienced having a father that I loved, I wasn't ready to let him go so soon.

My mind was very clear — this cancer was NOT going to take my father away from me!

I just needed a plan.

—— $$$ ——

I was pacing up and down in the hospital reception, racking my brains on how I could help, when I literally ran into a man and knocked him over. His coffee had spilt everywhere and I was most apologetic.

"That's OK," he said, "nothing will spoil my mood today, it's my fifth anniversary!"

"Fifth anniversary?" I asked, still trying to dab the coffee stains off his shirt with a tissue.

"Yes, I've been in remission from cancer for five years. I'm just in overnight for some tests to make sure I'm still all clear, but I know I am — I haven't felt this fit for decades!"

"Congratulations," I said with genuine admiration. "May I ask what type of cancer you had?"

"It got me here," he said, pointing to his throat.

Throat! The exact same place my father had it, and here was living proof that it could be beaten.

"What a coincidence," I said, with a beam on my face. "Can I ask you a favour?"

"Sure," he replied, with what seemed an even bigger smile — the type of smile you have when you're *really* happy to be alive.

"I have somebody I'd like you to meet."

After a bit of prodding and cajoling, the duty nurse allowed my father and my new friend to stay overnight in the same room together. It wasn't long before my father's natural affability and this man's delight at being alive had them chatting away like they were old mates. Visiting hours ended and I went home, sure in the belief that the Universe was on my side and Convergence was working for me again.

The next morning my new friend had gone but the impact he had made had not. My father was sitting up in bed, sucking on his orange juice and taking the herbal concoction I had left for him, swearing at how bad it tasted and make smart comments at the pretty nurse. I could tell he had found his will to live.

My new friend had left me a note saying, "If you ever need my help again, call this number," and I did, many times over the trying months ahead. Not for my father, he was determined, but for me, for strength and courage and motivation from a complete stranger the Universe had provided just in the nick of time.

Nine weeks later my father walked out of the hospital, free of cancer forever. He had won!

Never before had I been so grateful for the lessons I had learnt.

In the ensuing months we spent a lot of time together, and when we couldn't be together we talked on the phone.

I learnt all about my father, a man I had lived with all my life but had never known, and he learnt all about me. I discovered that he wanted a little farm so he could grow fresh produce for his cooking, and that he had always wanted to own a Mercedes Benz. I ordered a Mercedes straight away and hoped it would be here in time for his birthday, and we instantly started looking for his farm.

It wasn't long before I couldn't neglect things at work for much longer and so we were left to catch up by phone.

One night, as I was just about to hang up, he caught me and said, "Son" — I had never heard him call me that before, and I was so surprised I almost missed what he said next — "I just want you to know that I love you."

"I love you too, Dad," I said. "Talk to you soon!"

As I hung up, it occurred to me that was the first time we had ever said "I love you" to one another.

That was the last time we would ever speak.

In a strange twist of fate, my father fell over in the bathtub one night and hit his head. The aneurism killed him just before I got to the hospital.

I was so angry with him, God, the Universe and anybody else who got in the way for allowing this to happen to us. He had fought so hard, only to die from a stupid fall!

I busied myself in the funeral preparations, and booked a small chapel for his cremation and wrote a little speech.

I was about to learn something else about him. The little chapel had seats for 40, which I thought would be more than enough. Over 300 people came. Former work colleagues and staff, the state manager of the company he had worked for, friends from all over the country, people who had known him since before I was born ... And all of them knew what I had just recently discovered: that my father was a great man.

"He was incredibly proud of you," said one of his friends.

"I know."

Our new friend from the hospital was there and we discussed my anger and disappointment with what had happened.

"Peter," he said, "I have learnt to take each day as it comes. I am grateful just to wake up each day. I know losing your father hurts, and it's unfair how it happened, but imagine what would have happened if he hadn't got cancer — he'd be dead now and you would never have got to know him, and he would never have got to know you. He would have gone to his grave with him still angry at you and you still resenting him. What a gift that disease was for the both of you.

"Challenge creates character," he went on, "and you have become a much greater man in the short time I have known you, and in the short time you have known your father."

I thought about what our new friend had said for a long, long time, and many years later it came home to me how very lucky my father and I were to have been given those few short months together.

And it reminded me how perfectly in order life can be.

Lesson

Every event, good and bad, is part of our path. Challenge creates the character we need to fulfil our dreams. Everything is in perfect balance.

CHAPTER 18

In Which I Learn About O.P.M.

I had never been to a bloodstock auction before. It was all very exciting. The beautiful people, the rich and famous all came to see and be seen. A few even bought horses.

Hundreds of thousands were bid in minutes as the rich, the trainers and the just plain stupid vied for possession of these fine beasts.

I was here with my wealthy friend, my beautiful friend and my beautiful friend's mother, who fancied herself as a bit of a breeder.

My wealthy friend had his eye on one particularly magnificent horse, which he was now sizing up with his binoculars.

The moment came when the horse was led into the arena, prancing and kicking and tossing up the sand on the ground, snorting in disgust at such an indignity! You could tell this proud stallion was disgusted at having to participate in such a spectacle and it was clear that he found us all to be well beneath him.

The bidding started, and was well underway before I noticed that my wealthy friend had not even started. I was careful not to do anything that might be construed as a bid, as any amount I could afford had long since been passed, and I leaned in and whispered to my wealthy friend, "Have you changed your mind?"

"On the contrary," he replied, "this auction business is a game — remember that — never show your hand."

"How much are you prepared to pay?" I asked, despite the increasing irritation on my wealthy friend's face.

The figure he mentioned staggered me.

"You could buy a whole village for that amount, probably a small country!" I gasped.

"I only said that's how much I was *prepared* to pay. I will buy him for a lot less than that. Now shush up, will you!"

I sat back, well chided.

Eventually the bidding slowed down. It was obvious that even the audience were astounded at the latest bid, already a record, but from what I could pick up from the conversations going on around me, still a bargain for a horse with such fine breeding lines.

Finally we were down to the last bidder. Everybody else was exhausted and the auctioneer could not get another bid from anybody.

The final bidder stared intently and nervously at the auctioneer as the latter tried to coax one last bid out of the also-rans. His gaze was fixed as the auctioneer called, "Going once, going twice, third and final call, are we all done, are we all through?"

I swear I heard an "s" sound just as my wealthy friend called out his bid.

There was a gasp from the audience at the audacity of it.

The confidence with which it was put, the ringing strength of it, startled everybody, not the least the former bidder who thought he had won. My wealthy friend stood there casually and confidently, staring straight at him, and as the under bidder turned around it was obvious that he was rattled. The under bidder hesitated for some time as my wealthy friend continued to stare directly at him, then shook his head and walked away, his head hung in defeat.

And without a further bid, my wealthy friend had bought a horse.

Over Champagne I couldn't help but comment, "I know you have a lot of money, and I have seen many of your toys, but to pay that much for a horse, that was insane!"

"Well, Peter," he said, "then you don't know a good investment when you see one. Because of the price I just paid, the other 12 horses I own from the same sire have already gone up in value.

So much so, I guess their increase will more than pay for this one purchase. And look at that horse. Even at half pace, he could outrun most of the nags floating around. More importantly, he would hardly have to win a race and he would still be worth a fortune in stud fees."

"I see what you mean."

"Surely you know from your own investments that if you buy something of quality and put it to work for you earning an income, it will rise in value?"

"Umm, not really."

"What do you mean, not really?"

"Well, you see, I don't own any investments."

"What?" My wealthy friend was clearly shocked. "You've been earning good money for going on three years now, so what have you spent it all on?"

That was a question I had to think about. "Well, we have a new car, nice furniture, we've travelled."

"No, no, no!" he said, getting flushed in the cheeks. "Those things are meant to come *after* your investments."

"You never taught me that!"

"I just presumed," he said, "that everybody knew!"

I could feel a lecture coming on.

"You'll never be wealthy without putting money aside to invest in quality growth assets. Rich people always set aside money for their investments first and only spend anything they have left. It is the poor people who do it the other way around."

"But my business is doing well," I protested.

"So what are you going to do when it stops doing well, or you can't work or you get tired of what you are doing?

"Your business might be earning you an income, but income only equals lifestyle — assets equal wealth.

"Look at the wealthiest people in the country. Whenever you hear them talked about, people say, 'There goes "X", and he's worth millions.' They never say, 'There goes "X" who earns a lot.' How much are you *worth*?"

"Well, let's see," I said, "my clothes are worth about ... "

"No, sorry, those are depreciating items. They go down in value. Even though you may have spent money on them they have no real worth."

"OK, my furniture is worth ... "

"No, it depreciates too."

"Computers?"

"Nope."

"My car?"

"Not really."

"How about my business?"

"Maybe. Don't you own any property or shares?"

"No — I don't know where to start."

"Don't give me that," he said, suddenly irritated. "You know everything you need to know to invest. They same principles that I have taught you are universals — they apply to every activity. Take your friend's mother here. She was telling me before the auction that she bought and renovated a house and is about to sell it for a tidy profit. Wouldn't you call that creating uniqueness, adding value and applying leverage through appealing to people's emotions?"

"I guess so," I replied.

"It's no good working for an income," he went on. "You should only work for love.

"Your money should flow from your investments, so that you don't have to work. Too many people work because they have to, not because they want to. You have to get to a point where the income you receive from investing far exceeds the amount you spend each year. That's when you know you have achieved financial freedom. Only then can you call yourself rich.

"Take that horse of mine. He can earn me money through racing and we'll breed him at the same time. The mares we put him to will bear foals that, one day, will be worth as much as him. And the income I earn from that is essentially free. I could borrow every cent that I just paid for him and never pay it back, and the interest would only be a tiny fraction of what I would eventually be earning from that one asset."

"What if he fell over and broke his leg?" I joked, realising how stupid it sounded just as soon as I had said it.

"Then he is insured, and we get our money back.

"You can do this with houses too," he went on, not amused by my attempt at humour.

"What," I said, frowning, "breed them?"

"In a fashion. Let's say you buy a house — a good property that is going to grow in value — and you rent it out. As it grows in value, you gain what's called equity — the difference between what the property is worth and what you owe on it. You can use that equity to buy more houses. They too will grow in equity, and you can use that to buy even more, building your asset base and therefore your wealth."

"But I can't afford to buy a house," I protested.

"You don't pay for them yourself, you use O.P.M."

"O.P.M.?"

"Other people's money! Rich folk never use their own money when it is more effective to use somebody else's. O.P.M. is the ultimate leverage! But you've got to remember that leverage can work for you or against you. If you borrow money to buy a house that goes up in value, you magnify your profits ... But if it goes down in value, you magnify your losses.

"Using O.P.M. is like using any other leverage. There is a right way and a wrong way. Most people borrow money to buy things that go down in value, like your clothes, furniture and car. What they don't realise is that the same repayments they are making on those items would probably pay for a house. You see, the rent on a good property should pay off most of the interest and costs and you only have to make up the rest.

"Quality property doubles in value every 10 years or so. That means if you borrow to buy a house that's worth $100,000 today, even if you only pay back the interest, you will have equity of $100,000 after 10 years. If you have 10 houses you will be a millionaire, all using O.P.M.

"Rich people only ever borrow money when the amount they will make from the investment will exceed the amount they have

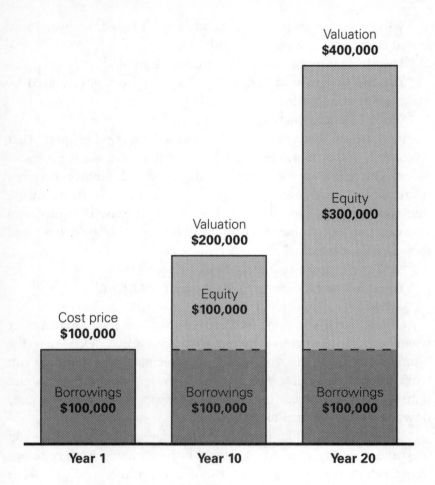

Quality property should double in value every 10 years

to pay in interest. This way you are making a profit or gaining equity. And the good news is that there is always heaps of money to lend!

"As long as you master the skill of using borrowed funds properly, and only ever use it buy assets that will grow in value more than the interest you are paying, it's the easiest way to become rich.

"Ordinary people kill their chances of ever becoming rich by sapping their resources with debts for things that go down in value.

"Over time, as the value of good properties goes up, so does the rent. It won't be long before the properties are paying for themselves and you are also earning an income from them. If you keep on buying more property, eventually the income you get from them will exceed the amount you spend. Then you will be rich!

"But who would lend me money?" I asked.

"Why, the banks of course."

I didn't want to remind him that I had only just been discharged from bankruptcy a year ago, but I knew I would never get the answer if I didn't ask the question.

"Yes, I forgot about that," he said, "but the good news is, so will the banks, eventually. But for now you will have to find private finance."

"You mean, like you?" I asked hopefully.

"Never a money lender be, young man, and especially not to your friends. Friends are hard to find, money is not. Private lenders are individuals or groups of people who lend money to people who may not meet the banks' criteria. You will have to pay a higher interest rate than the banks but, as long as your rent plus your capital growth always exceeds your costs and interest, you will be in front. Be very careful with the contracts, some of them are sharks, but there are more than enough who are ethical and good to deal with. Eventually, when you build up a good enough credit rating with the private lenders, the banks will fund you again."

It was time to go borrow some money.

(*Note*: This was in the era prior to the deregulation of the banking industry. There are now thousands of lenders who will loan money to anybody as long as they are not an undischarged bankrupt. There are also special loans called no-doc and low-doc loans for people who have difficulty proving their income or have a low income but large asset base. Heed my wealthy friend's advice though: be careful to ensure you understand exactly the terms of the loan and make sure any investment you make is going to grow in value and return you an income that will be more than the costs associated with the loan.)

Lesson

Rich people borrow money when the amount they will make from the investment will exceed the amount they have to pay in interest. Master the skill of using borrowed funds properly, to buy assets that will grow in value more than the interest you are paying.

Your money should flow from your investments, so that you don't have to work. Too many people work because they have to, not because they want to. You have to get to a point where the income you receive from investing far exceeds the amount you spend each year. That's when you know you have achieved financial freedom. Only then can you call yourself rich.

CHAPTER 19

In Which I Buy a House or Two

My first house purchase was a tiny little two-bedroom about five blocks from the beach. It cost me $26,000 when the average price for a house in the district was about $100,000. I spent $6,000 on a purely cosmetic rejuvenation — paint, polishing the timber floors, fixing bits and pieces, and so on — and I sold it for $40,000 nine weeks after buying. I had made $8,000! That's more than I had made in nine months at the supermarket.

This became a hobby for me. I would find a house, do it up and sell it. It was lots of fun and I was making good money.

Eventually, my wealthy friend pointed out the folly of my ways.

"There are only three reasons a rich person ever sells anything," he said. "The first is that they don't want it any more. The reason the item was purchased has changed, it is no longer in use, or it is being upgraded.

"The second is that they are offered an obscene amount of money for it — much more than it is actually worth and even better if there is a pretty good chance that they will be able to buy it back again shortly at a much lower price. This happens all the times during booms — people paying over the money for things — property, shares, and trophy items. And busts can come. But they must also be prepared to sacrifice that asset, maybe never to see it again, and the price must be extraordinary.

"And the third reason a rich person sells is that they made a mistake in their purchase. Their research was wrong, or they misjudged the timing or price, or there is a dramatic change in circumstances. It takes a big person to swallow their pride, admit

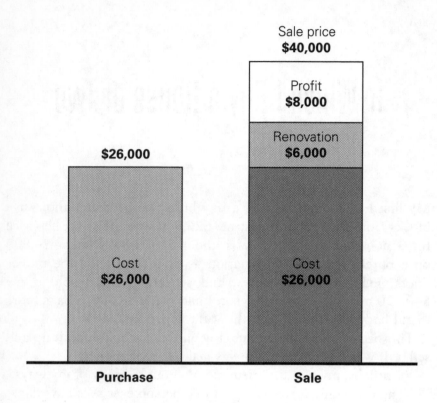

My first house purchase and sale

their mistake and sell a 'dog' investment so that they can free up their money to invest in something worthwhile.

"Other than that, the rich accumulate but they only buy things of value. Some of my friends have lived for years during the bad times by quietly selling off the items of value they have accumulated over the years until things get good again!

"They rarely buy anything that is unlikely to increase in value or at least maintain its value. They are always patient in their purchasing. Most buying mistakes are made because of impatience. A colleague has the saying, 'The deal of a lifetime comes along about twice a week!' meaning it is rare that an 'opportunity' passed up won't represent itself in exactly the same or a different form.

"Ordinary people overspend, then justify their poor purchasing and money control by saying things like, 'It was on sale', or 'It was a bargain', or 'I can use this so many times' when they didn't need it, it wasn't that cheap and they only used it once! Rich people wait until they can afford exactly what they want, and then they find the most leveraged, tax effective and intelligent way to buy it.

"Contrary to popular opinion, rich people rarely pay cash for anything, even toys and indulgences. If there is a way it can be financed that doesn't drain cash flow and which frees money up for investment, or if there is a way that the risk of a purchase can be shared or minimised by using other people's money or involving others in the project, rich people will take that option.

"But they know never to over-extend themselves. Rich people know the easiest way to get poor is to over-extend, to take on projects that are too big a risk, to borrow too much money at too high an interest rate. And this judgment is what distinguishes rich people from ordinary people. Rich people know how to use leverage without over-extending, how to judge and take risks, but not risk it all or too much.

"But most of all, rich people don't sell quality assets. Take that very first house of yours that you sold. Did you get a good price for it?"

"Of course I did — 35% more than I bought it for," I replied.

"And your return after costs?"

"Still a handsome profit of 20%."

"Not a bad return indeed. But tell me something, how many properties have you bought and sold over the last couple of years?"

I had to think. "About 50 or so."

"That's a lot of property."

"What would have happened if you had kept them?"

"Well, for starters I wouldn't have got the profit by selling them," I replied, still justifying my position.

"That's true, but think about it, how many of those properties were worth keeping? In other words, which of them were top-quality purchases?"

"Well, most I think."

"And how long did it take you to find each of those properties?"

I knew the answer to that one. "A long time!"

I had been out looking at property just about every Thursday and Saturday for the last three years, wearing out my welcome with dozens of real-estate agents, getting out my measuring tape, crawling under houses with my torch, turning on taps and flushing toilets, negotiating on price and bidding at auction, then stripping, painting, polishing and presenting . . .

Now that I thought about it, it was damn hard work. First in finding the properties and then in doing them up.

"Well," he said, "imagine if you had spent that time accumulating, how many properties do you think you could have kept out of the ones you sold?"

I shrugged my shoulders. "I guess about a third."

"So you reckon you could have kept a third, hey? Well, if those 17 properties were worth $200,000 each, and they grew at just 10% each year for the last three years, you would now have $1,125,000 in equity. In other words, you would be a *millionaire* by now. Wasn't that one of your goals?"

"Umm, yes it was," I replied, chastised as usual.

"And how much did you actually make by buying and selling all these houses?"

I had to work it out, but the answer surprised and embarrassed me. After I paid all the expenses, stamp duty, agents' fees, advertising, legals, renovation costs, and tax, it came to a little over $250,000 net. It seemed a lot at the time but the expenses had really eaten into my profits, especially the dastardly tax.

"So," said my wealthy friend in a manner in which I knew he was about to deliver yet another lesson, "not only did you buy and sell almost $10 million in property and only make 2.5% on your money, you gave up a third of the potential properties by selling them all and not holding on to any."

"Mmm, I guess so."

"And where is that money now?"

"I don't know."

"Exactly," he said, with a raised eyebrow.

"Quality assets held for the long term will make you rich. It doesn't matter how big your income is, if you don't put some of it aside to invest you will never be rich. Rich people make their money work like slaves so they don't have to.

"Learn to live on 70% of your income. Put the rest to work for you. If you can't live on 70%, then live on 80%. If you can't do that, live on 90%. If you can't do that, for goodness' sake live on 99% and at least put 1% towards your future, and work up to 70%. Remember, you know you are rich when your income generated by your investments exceeds your expenditure on everything you need, want and desire in your life. Eventually you will be living on a fraction of your income. In fact, you won't be able to spend everything you earn."

"Now that would be amazing," I said, "because I want to spend a lot!"

"If you ever want to be rich, it's time you stopped selling and started accumulating."

Lesson

You'll know you are rich when your income generated by your investments exceeds your expenditure. Learn to live on 70% of your income, and put the rest towards accumulating assets that will appreciate. Wealth comes from accumulating quality assets held for the long term.

CHAPTER 20

The Three Key Elements of all Investments

We were standing in the garage of a mechanic who looked old enough to have been around at the invention of the first car. While tinkering under the bonnet of my wealthy friend's classic 1954 Aston Martin, he kept muttering something about how silly these "new" things were.

I couldn't figure why on earth my wealthy friend would actually come down here himself when he had so many staff, including a full-time chauffeur who looked after all his cars, classic or not.

Little did I know that a lesson in investing was waiting for me dressed in the guise of a grease monkey.

"Do you mind showing my young friend your sign, Oliver?"

"Yup," said the mechanic, not looking up from the perfectly clean but roughly idling engine.

"Well, we'll just look at it ourselves then, OK?" said my wealthy friend, with a tone that led me to believe he was expecting that answer.

"Yup," said the mechanic, adjusting some thingumajig.

My wealthy friend showed me the way, dodging old engine and suspension parts strewn on the floor of the workshop, to Oliver's office, where, in amongst girly pictures of movie stars from long ago, there was a tattered sign that read:

SPEED, QUALITY, PRICE — PICK ANY 2.

"It's exactly the same with investing," said my wealthy friend. "There are three things to look out for:

"*Growth* — in other words, the asset goes up in value over time.

"*Income* — in other words, the asset produces a cash return in the form of dividends, rent or interest.

"And *low risk* — in other words, the potential of losing your money is low."

"It's virtually impossible to get all three in the one investment.

"If you go for high growth but low risk, then you will probably have to sacrifice income.

"If you want income and low risk, then you will probably have to sacrifice growth.

"And if you want income and high growth, then you will have to accept a higher level of risk.

"There is no investment without some level of risk. The higher the return, the higher the risk — this is an absolute given. Anybody who tells you otherwise is lying, but that doesn't mean to say that you have to give up growth and income entirely.

"Rich people know that there are ways to get a good-quality investment that will outperform the ordinary and still maintain and manage an acceptable risk. There are always ways to manage the risks in an investment — you just have to brush up on your skills and knowledge.

"People are constantly trying to go for high income or growth and their common sense is blinded by the promise of a big return. So many people do their dough on dodgy investments that have a good 'front' but promise ridiculously high returns with little or no risk.

"Rich people are prepared to take some risk, they have to, but they always have risk management in place. They might spread their investments around a little bit, making sure they have a bit of property and a bit of shares, while maintaining a small emergency fund. They make sure that they buy shares in quality companies and monitor their performance. They might have one or two higher-risk investments but it will always be in something they understand and it will always be only a small percentage of their funds.

"So," I said, "it's OK to take a few risks, but I should make sure that I spread it around and only ever risk a small amount on high-growth or income-potential investments and that I should do this only if I understand them?"

"Absolutely," he said. "People get sucked in to investing in things they don't understand. The classic 'stings' always involve gullible investors, whatever their level of education, as well as 'new' and 'unique' ways of investing, the promise of high returns and low risk. The scammers always have a spiel that sounds completely logical, and if they throw in some supposed tax benefits, they have a winning scam formula.

"Unfortunately, these scams come up every year in different forms and no matter how hard the legislators try, they will never catch up with all of them, so it is up to you as an individual investor to ensure that you know what you are investing in and are comfortable with the risks."

"So which of the three items should I take? Growth, income or low risk?" I asked.

"Well, it depends. Property has lower growth than shares, but you can get much higher leverage by borrowing to buy and it has lower risk in the short term. Shares have higher income and growth than property, but are slightly higher risk that property in the short term. You need to have a balance.

"Most rich people are actually quite conservative investors — they got rich by buying quality assets with good growth potential and holding on to them, but what's the fun of assets if you don't have any income at all? Most rich people I know, outside their businesses if they own them, have pretty even amounts tied up in property and shares. The property provides the vast majority of the growth in the portfolio because of the leverage. The shares provide an opportunity for good growth, some income and diversification. And sometimes they might have a small kitty, never more than 10% of their assets, set aside for higher-risk investments. And if they were ever to 'blow' that 10%, they would need to make back three times that amount before they would put anything into the high-risk area again.

"Just remember that all investments carry risk and you must learn how to manage those risks. But if you don't invest, you'll never be rich.

"The critical thing is to have a plan. Rich people always have a Wealth Creation Plan — written down, fully expanded and with detailed outcomes, so they know they are on track.

"So, Peter, how many properties do you *plan* to buy this year?"

I had never thought about that before. I just bought them as I got around to it, when I had some spare time away from my business and had some spare cash left over.

"OK, well I'm going to buy six then."

"That's a great goal," said my wealthy friend, "but let's make it even easier. How much money do you need as a deposit for each property?"

I gave him a figure.

"Excellent. That doesn't seem like a large amount of money does it?"

"Well, I'll have to work a bit but I think I can do it."

"How about, instead of saying you are going to buy six properties, have as your plan getting as many of those deposits as you can. Set about getting the deposit and then just buy a property. Every time you get a deposit from anywhere — cash or equity — buy an investment property. Put your head down and go for it. I don't want you to do any adding up of your wealth or counting your assets without me. I'm off to Provence for a year, so that'll give you enough time to put your plan into action. We'll catch up when I get back and we'll see how you've done."

"You could bring me back a beret," I suggested.

Lesson

A wealth creation plan must address the three key elements of investing, which are growth, income and low risk, but it's virtually impossible to get all three in the one investment. All investments carry some risk — but if you don't invest, you'll never be rich — so learn how to manage risk, and never invest in something if you don't understand it.

CHAPTER 21

In Which I Invent "Leapfrogging"

All my buying and selling of property had taught me something . . .

There is money to be made by value adding. The little renovations that I did, always nothing more than cosmetic touch-ups, had virtually always meant that I made a good profit when it came time to sell.

It was very simple — I would use the *leverage* of borrowing to buy a property.

At first I had to use private lenders and pay a premium for borrowing money, but they were very flexible and were not worried that I'd had some defaults in the past. Eventually I was able to use cheaper methods of financing as my credit rating improved.

I would then *value add* to the property by making it more cosmetically appealing. I selected properties that were structurally sound but a bit run down. I would paint them and decorate them, using a bit of flair, getting my ideas from books and magazines that always had tips on the best and cheapest ways to renovate. This, of course, added *uniqueness*, and my properties were always popular when I came to sell them.

Now it was time to find out if they were popular to tenants as well.

My first project was an apartment in a fashionable area. I gathered together as many trendy magazines as I could to get ideas, and even though there were certainly some wild and wacky things in there, I did know that it was vital for me to renovate to my potential market's taste and not my own.

After a quick coat of paint, some new carpets, some flashy bits and pieces like door handles and some refinishing work on the bathroom and kitchen we were ready for rental D-Day. In those days I used to rent out my properties myself (until too many years of 3.00 a.m. phone calls from tenants complaining about something that could have waited till 8.00 a.m. cured me of that). I dressed up in my Sunday best, put some cookies in the oven and some lemon scent in the bathroom, and waited for my first customers.

To say that I was overwhelmed would be an understatement. I used all my best adjectives in the ads and I obviously undercharged for the rent (even though I had put it up by over 50% from pre-renovation days), because I had 27 people through and got six applications to be my first tenants.

My beautiful friend suggested that I get them a house-warming present (something I still do to this day — and anniversary presents and Christmas presents to thank my tenants for looking after my properties for me — I don't really know what difference it makes, but my properties certainly do seem to stay rented longer than those owned by most of my friends).

I can't describe to you how proud and excited I was to have my very own tenant. I even had a photo taken of me handing over the keys! And even though I now own dozens of properties, I still sometimes sneak out and go driving past as many as I can, just to remind myself how far I've come.

I remembered what my wealthy friend said about getting my next deposit. He said, "As soon as you've got it from anywhere — cash or equity — go buy your next property." So, I thought, it was time to get my brand-new tenanted apartment revalued by the bank.

I certainly expected a bigger fanfare. I had helped the tenant clean the property and it was sparkling. I even loaned them some bits and pieces and decorator items (which had always helped me to get a higher price when I was selling), then I dressed up in my Sunday best again, and waited.

The bank valuer took one look at the outside of my little

apartment and asked me how much it rented for. I told him, he added three zeros to the end — and that was my valuation!

I asked him how he came to that figure so quickly, without even seeing inside.

"Straight return," he said.

"Huh?" I asked, trying not to sound too dumb.

"A $100,000 property rents for $100 a week, so if your property rents for $250 a week, it's worth $250,000."

That rule of thumb was to make me a lot of money over the years!

(Since then, I have certainly become more sophisticated in influencing the valuation in my favour over the years, and I would never allow a valuer to do such a brief "thumbnail" valuation these days, but at least his method was better than the "drive by" valuations I have seen some do.)

The valuer gave me a piece of paper that was more valuable than any piece of paper I'd had before. That valuation allowed me to go back to the bank and draw down the equity I had added into the property by doing the renovation. So not only had the bank loaned me the money to buy the property and loaned me the money to do the renovation, they were now going to loan me the money to buy my next property. I certainly loved this "leverage"!

My wealthy friend once commented that it was like the game the children play, leaping over other children who were crouching down, so they could get ahead, so I called my new strategy "Leapfrogging", and this is how it's done:

- use equity or cash as the first deposit;
- rejuvenate to add value (cosmetic renovations only);
- increase the rent (it's important to do this before the revaluation because the increase in the rent helps justify the new higher valuation you are going to ask for the property);
- have the property revalued;
- refinance to draw down equity for your next deposit;
- buy your next property and rejuvenate.

"Leapfrogging" allows you to buy property continuously without deposits, as long as you can continue to service the loans (the tenant and the tax man help you with this, by paying off most of the costs).

So, as an example, say you bought a property for $200,000 that was structurally sound but a bit "tired" and spent $20,000 doing it up.

If renovated properties in that area are going for $250,000 you should be able to get $250 to $280 a week in rent for your property and it will be worth $250,000.

This means that you will have made $30,000! Depending on your deposit requirement for your loan, the bank will allow you to draw down a certain proportion of that equity, which should be enough for your second property. So your second property costs you nothing out of your own pocket.

Your interest will be about $290 per week (at 7%) and so it will only cost you between $10 and $40 a week to own.

If you set up the loan correctly you can claim tax deductions as well, lowering the cost even further!

That means you can keep on buying properties as long as you can afford the $40 per property each week.

What do you do when you run out of $40s per week? Well, the not-so-obvious answer is "earn more", but if that is absolutely impossible, you just wait ...

Wait until the rent has gone up and the property is paying for itself.

As an example, let's say that you could afford $120 a week, or three properties.

You have to find your first deposit, but from then on your deposits come out of increased equity that you have made through value adding. So that means properties 2 and 3 don't cost you anything out of your pocket for the deposit and so effectively become free!

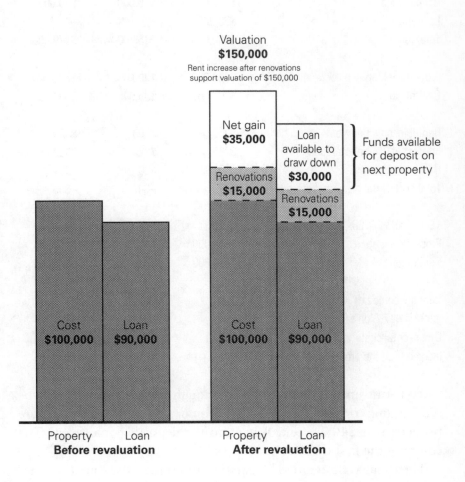

Valuation
$150,000

Rent increase after renovations
support valuation of $150,000

Net gain
$35,000

Loan
available to
draw down
$30,000

Renovations
$15,000

Renovations
$15,000

} Funds available
for deposit on
next property

Cost
$100,000

Loan
$90,000

Cost
$100,000

Loan
$90,000

Property   Loan
Before revaluation

Property   Loan
After revaluation

Leapfrogging

LEAPFROGGING

	1st Property	2nd Property	3rd Property
Property cost	$200,000	$150,000	$250,000
Renovations	$20,000	$15,000	$20,000
Less: cash deposit	$20,000	–	–
Total loan	$200,000	$165,000	$270,000
Property valuation after renovations	$250,000	$200,000	$320,000
Capital gain	$30,000	$35,000	$50,000
Rental income per week	$250	$200	$320
Interest at 7% on total loan	$269	$222	$363
Other rental costs	$20	$20	$20
Total cost of the property before tax	–$39	–$42	–$63
TEN YEARS LATER			
Property valuation	$500,000	$400,000	$640,000
Capital gain	$280,000	$235,000	$370,000
Rental income per week	$500	$400	$640
Interest at 7% on total loan	$269	$222	$363
Other rental costs	$40	$40	$40
Income from the property before tax	$191	$138	$237

You wait until the rent goes up enough for the properties to be self-funding (or cash flow neutral). You can then afford three more properties at $40 a week. Where do the deposits come from? The equity in the first three!

Then you wait again. The exciting thing is in your next 'round' of buying you can now afford six properties — because not only are the first three paying for themselves, they should now be making $40 a week each in profit because the rents should have gone up, so your buying capacity magnifies.

This is the excitement of leverage. Of course it doesn't always work perfectly, sometimes you will get a little less, which means you have to wait a bit longer for the growth and rental increases, sometimes a little more, which means you can move quicker, but whatever happens you should be way in front.

Now we know that well-selected property should double in value every 10 years or so, so in a decade that original property will be worth $500,000 and — even if you haven't paid off a cent of the loan (only interest) — you will have made $250,000 in equity out of thin air! And by this stage your rent should have increased to between $500 and $550 a week, giving you an income of $210 to $260 a week. Not bad, and it sure beats working for a crust!

I soon got the hang of leapfrogging and I followed my wealthy friend's advice. As soon as I had enough for another deposit, either through cash, which I managed to save up or extract from my business profits, or equity that I got from my value adding, I bought another property.

My progress was rapid, and I couldn't wait for the return of my wealthy friend!

Lesson

Leapfrogging allows you to buy properties continuously without deposits, as long as you can continue to service the loans (the tenant and the tax man can help you with this, by paying off most of the costs). The more your equity and rents grow, the more properties you can acquire!

CHAPTER 22

In Which I Discover I am a Millionaire

"Come up to the farm for the weekend, and we'll add up your wealth," said my wealthy friend.

I couldn't wait. Not only because I had never been to his "farm" — which is how he referred to his horse stud — and I was sure it would be a treat, but because I had stayed true to my promise and had not "counted my wealth". Of course I had a good idea that I had done well, but had not quantified it.

I had armed myself with my bank loan statements, valuations and rental assessments, and I was keen to learn how close I had come to my goal of being a millionaire.

"We'll be flying up," said my wealthy friend.

"Which airline?" I asked.

"Oh, we'll be flying in our own plane."

Well, that was embarrassing, I thought, better stick to a safer question.

"How long will that take?" I asked.

"It depends on which plane we take," my wealthy friend said, with only a hint of irony.

When I was a kid I wanted to be a Navy pilot, and although I couldn't become one because I needed glasses, I'd always loved aviation and dreamt of one day owning a private jet of my very own.

I pulled straight up to the car park in front of the hangar, and walked straight onto the plane. It was sleek and luxurious. The leading edge of its wings glistened in the sun, and as soon as I'd sunk into a leather chair and fastened my seatbelt, they pulled the door closed behind me and we took off straight away.

A beautiful attendant served me gourmet seafood and fluffed a little pillow behind my back for the short flight to my wealthy friend's horse stud.

I gotta get me one of these, I thought. No check in, no luggage restrictions, no waiting around in overcrowded lounges for an inevitably late flight, and no horrible reheated meals served by disinterested flight attendants.

The plane touched down on the private airstrip on my wealthy friend's property. I could see white post-and-rail fences, and modern buildings designed to blend in with the late 19th-century sandstone buildings that were the original dwellings on the property.

It was obvious that a *lot* of money had been lavished on this property. Giant irrigation sprinklers were spraying water over pure green, almost manicured paddocks, and beautiful horses of every nature and colour were running free. A huge polo field with its own grandstand was hosting a game for local children taking their introduction to horse sports very seriously. Cheers went out as points were scored.

Of all my wealthy friend's possessions, this surely was the most impressive.

"You'll be staying in the guest cottage," he said, greeting me at the airstrip. "Let me take you up there." We jumped into a jeep which looked so daggy and old that I half expected to have to jump out and crank start it!

As we approached the building compound, I saw the main house — a two-storey Georgian mansion, immaculately restored, but not as large as I imagined. As we pulled up, there was somebody sweeping the front step.

"This is Greg," said my wealthy friend. "He'll look after you while you are staying with us."

My wealthy friend took me on a tour. The house was lavishly decorated with the finest antiques, paintings, carvings and finishes. For somebody who loved old houses as I did, it was fascinating to see the attention to detail that had gone into the restoration, including detailed gold filigree work, original-looking black and white tiles, and a glorious Victorian round dining table that would seat eight.

The house had five bedrooms and a study. It was perfectly clean, no doubt due to the attentions of Greg the butler, but somehow looked unlived in.

"Wow, it's great," I said at the end of the tour, "but somehow I expected it to be a bit bigger."

"Why, are you expecting guests yourself?"

All of a sudden I realised that this wasn't the main house — this was the guest cottage!

"The main house is on the other side of the hill. Let's go up and have some supper."

Now, *this* was a house! Twelve bedrooms, indoor swimming pool, sauna and spa, billiard room, separate wings for the guests and children, servants' quarters, a whopping big kitchen and the pièce de résistance, a ballroom, which was a hive of activity.

"We're having a small party tomorrow night, to celebrate a birthday. I do hope you brought your dinner suit!"

I didn't even own a dinner suit!

For the next two days a party atmosphere filled the house, and although I was keen to "do the maths" on my wealth creation, my wealthy friend had neither the time nor inclination to sit down with me, so I settled back and enjoyed the atmosphere.

The "small party" had a guest list of just 300 or so people. Food, drink and entertainment flowed freely, with weary guests going home or staying in one of the many cottages spread out over the property. The children slept in one great shed called the "ringer's quarters". I was immensely jealous that I was too old to share in what must have been the most amazing pyjama party!

Sunday lunch was a casual affair with only close family and friends. Still, there were well over three-dozen people sitting down to a meal served on a long pine table in the shade of a peppercorn tree.

This is the life, I mused to myself. And I realised it wasn't necessarily the money, although this certainly was a fabulous setting for a BBQ. On second thoughts, it didn't really matter that much about the setting. The important thing was that everybody was happy to be together and they were having fun. This could have occurred on this multi-million dollar property, or it could have been in a local park.

It struck me that people today are so busy trying to make an income, they have forgotten what simple pleasures there can be had in just being with people you love and who love you in a fun atmosphere where the last thing on anybody's mind is work.

I fell asleep on the veranda in a lazy chair while watching the kids, some not so little, play a game of touch football on the lawn.

"Come on, sleepy head," my wealthy friend said, as he gently shook me awake, "it's time to go sit in our counting house and count out all your money."

We sat around his antique partner's desk in his study, and I was quite excited as I poured all my papers onto the desk. I wonder how far I had to go to my goal. Maybe I had even passed it?

In the 12 months since our last meeting, I had managed to accumulate an additional 11 properties. Added to the five I had kept of my old properties, plus my own house, that made a total of 17 properties.

We added up all the valuations on the properties and they came to $4,850,000. We added up all the outstanding loans and costs on the properties, and they came to $3,637,500. With a few other investments and other things I owned, I had another $100,000 in assets. That made my net worth $1,312,500!

"Congratulations," said my wealthy friend, "you are a millionaire!"

I was stunned. In just over four years since leaving the supermarket, I had built up a small but respectable fortune of over a million dollars. *I'd done it!*

I sat there for quite some time not saying anything. My wealthy friend didn't say anything either. We just sat in silence on his green leather chairs, soaking up the feeling of a person savouring a major achievement.

After a suitable time, my wealthy friend said, "No matter what happens in your life from now on, nobody can take this away from you. Although many people talk about becoming wealthy, you've gone and done it. But let's not make this your finest hour. There is a lot more — much, much more — for you to do yet."

As I sat in my wealthy friend's plane on my way home, I started to write a new list of things to achieve: people to meet, objects to own, challenges to overcome, dreams to bring into reality ...

Lesson

Dreams can be brought into reality with the right plan, focus and application.

CHAPTER 23

In Which I Ignore all the Warnings and Overstretch

Wealth was good.

It certainly was good to have what I wanted, not to have to worry where my next meal was coming from and to enjoy a few luxuries in life.

But, like most people who make a million dollars and realise that it isn't that much, I wanted more.

It was hard to keep up the pace of my first years in property, and although my wealthy friend encouraged me to keep on going at a sensible pace, I didn't even have the material things on my original list. I seemed to be so close and yet so far.

I thought that maybe my skills were ready for a challenge.

"Why ask for challenge?" my wealthy friend questioned. "Ask for an easy life."

"Mmm, but I'm bored, I need something to get my teeth into."

"Well, take up a hobby! Money is not the place to look for excitement. Too many people look to investing as a thrill, but really it's quite boring. If you are following a strategy, you are really just doing the same things over and over again. And this is what develops your skills. As you develop skills, you are able to get better and better at squeezing more and more margin for less effort."

"I understand all that, but things are going too slowly."

"You mean zero to one million dollars in four years is too slow? Most people don't make that much money in a lifetime!"

"Hey, don't give me that," I replied, getting irritated, "you're the one who said don't compare yourself to the ordinary."

"I did indeed, 'Ordinary is where the cream of the crap meets the crap of the cream.'"

"Well then, if I'm ever truly going to get ahead, I'm going to have to do more than this."

"Be careful, Peter, I've warned you about overstretching. Ordinary people are always chasing the big score, the big win, but there's no such thing. Rich people know that wealth comes from persistently following a quality income and investment strategy."

"Now wait a second," I said, butting in. "You've told me heaps of times about your big wins where one of your investments has gone crazy and made you a fortune!"

"That's true, but it was also just good luck, and you should never rely on luck for your fortune. If good luck occurs, that's only a bonus."

"Don't worry — I'll plan well," I said. Famous last words!

The project was a big one — 22 units on a block of land facing the coast. Unit prices had been going up in the area for some time. I knew I was probably cutting it a bit fine, but the project could be built quickly.

The interest payments would really stretch my cash flow, but each apartment had $100,000 to $150,000 profit in it, so that would mean I could make close to $3,000,000 profit from one deal. The banks wouldn't consider the finance, as they thought it was too much for me to take on. I had made $2,000,000 in equity in the last few years but it was all tied up, so I asked my beautiful friend's mother if I could use her property as security for the loan. I agreed to give her 50% of the profit and "wear" any losses.

The type of apartment that was popular in the area was big, brick and boring. People seemed to want size over style, but I thought there would be a market for something a little different. My apartments wouldn't be as big as the others, but they'd have far better quality finishes and fittings.

The builder set to work.

We had a problem with the excavation, so the builder suggested that instead of going down we fill the block and go up. I couldn't see any problem with that, especially as it would give the apartments a better view of the beach.

Everything was going very well. The buildings were to lock-up stage on time and we started trying to sell off the plan.

Lots of people came to inspect, but when they saw the size of the apartments and realised they only had one garage instead of two they didn't stay. I really thought that once they saw the quality, they would buy.

In the meantime, the interest rates started going up and I had counted on about half of the units being sold by now. Cash flow in the business was getting tight. We needed money for marketing campaigns, but we didn't have it, so things got tighter still. That was nothing compared to the next problem though.

When the council inspector came he called a halt to the work, stating that the building exceeded the height limit for the area and would block the view from the property behind.

As we were only a couple of weeks away from finishing, I was surprised to say the least. "How on earth could the building exceed the height limit?" I asked. "You approved the plan."

"I didn't approve *that*," he replied, pointing to the area the builder had filled instead of excavated. "This building is 1.8 metres higher than shown on the plans you submitted to the council."

"What do you want me to do? Take the roof off?" I asked, totally exasperated.

"You might have to," was his only reply.

And we did.

The council sued us, we sued the builder, while all the time the interest was mounting up and other builders were getting the jump on us. All of a sudden our innovative project was looking a little bit odd, especially when the council tried to force us to put a flat roof on the property when originally it had a 45° pitch on it. The court ordered that we would have to reduce the pitch of the roof to 30°, so off came the roof and down came the rain.

There is nothing more depressing than seeing your brand-new expensive kitchens, bathrooms, polished floors and designer fittings being rained on as builders try to get tarps to cover them.

The damage was horrendous, and some items had to be completely replaced.

We had to go back to the financiers and ask for an extension.

Eventually we did sell all the units — at an average loss of $80,000. I lost $1,800,000 in nine months.

These losses and others like it have taught me a lot.

My wealthy friend said, "It is the law of personal development that we are doomed to forever repeat our mistakes until we understand the lesson they are teaching us. It pays us well to deeply analyse our mistakes to discover what lessons they hold for us."

One of my greatest challenges is to always balance my vision with my skills. This lesson has come up many times for me. Hopefully I am closer each time to mastering it.

Today I stick to my Leapfrogging Strategy. It has allowed me to accumulate just over 100 properties in 10 years. Not bad for a former check-out chick.

Lesson

There is no such thing as "the big score". Wealth comes from persistently following a quality income and investment strategy and developing our skill level in applying it. Overstretching our skills and resources can easily lead to failure.

CHAPTER 24

In Which I "Brave" the Share Market for the First Time

My wealthy friend had brought me to see the trading floor at the Stock Exchange. It was very exciting ... People running to and fro, waving pieces of paper at each other, picking up phones and communicating by what seemed like indecipherable hand signals.

(There are very few working trading floors left. If you get the opportunity, do see one before they are all taken over by direct computer processing.)

Even though I had done quite well in property, I really didn't a have a clue about shares at this stage.

I had bought a few shares based on a "hot tip" from one of my friends. My wealthy friend had just sniggered when I mentioned them to him, but I just thought he was being old fashioned and couldn't see a good opportunity when I knew one! Of course, they performed abysmally. So largely I had stayed away from buying more shares, but my wealthy friend had convinced me to take another look as he had at least half his assets in the share market and had made a lot of profit over the years.

"Look at all that activity," commented my wealthy friend. "Every few seconds billions of dollars are traded around the world. If you stick your hand out long enough, some of it has to stick!

"Investing in the share market will reveal your true relationship to money. It is a harsh, bitter, swift and ruthless teacher of human character. Any greed you display will quickly be corrected in the market by loss. Any hesitation will quickly be destroyed by missed opportunity. Any error in judgment will quickly be magnified. Discipline and foresight is the key to this game.

"Look up at that board," he said, pointing to the green and red monitor displaying all the share prices. "That's like a destination board at the airport: every time it ticks over, a plane is sent out to gain or loss. Every time this board ticks over, a fortune is made and lost. But if you are disciplined and show foresight, your gains will outweigh your losses and multiply your wealth."

"Yes," I said, "but how do you pick companies from all those up there? Should I get myself a broker or adviser?"

"You don't need fancy advisers or some academic analyst — even though some of them are excellent — most of them confine their services to the ultra-rich, and finding those who don't is almost impossible. You simply need to educate yourself. There is nobody on the planet who will take more care of your money than you — just make sure that you are up to the task!"

I had never had anybody say that to me before ...

"You mean I could be a better manager of my funds than those big banks and investment houses?"

"Absolutely. Blind Freddy has a better chance of doing well in the markets than some of those folk. They might be big and they might do OK but, by the time you pay all their fees and charges, most of your profits disappear. How do you think they got such spectacular offices in the first place? The average person knows much more about what to invest in than they give themselves credit for. They just allow themselves to get 'blinded by science' by the people in the money industry. Do you remember that big float flop a couple of months ago?"

The company had received major newspaper and TV attention when it decided to float — the company was an icon and was supported heavily by the big broking houses. Many "Ma and Pa" investors bought in and most of them lost a lot of money as the company ended up trading at a figure far below what they had purchased the shares for.

"All I had to do was ask my wife and I knew not to buy into that float."

"What do you mean?" I asked.

"Well, she had shopped there for years and she told me that their service was going down hill, their stores looked tired and their competitors were doing it better. I didn't need any fancy broking house to tell me what my wife already knew just by being a customer of the business — it was going down hill and it would take the share price with it. Sure, they might be able to recover, but that takes time, resources and money.

"So even though my wife didn't have a degree or wasn't a highly trained analyst, she would have known to avoid those shares by just listening to her instinct.

"Most people think picking shares is some highly mystical science, but really it's good common sense. People make mistakes in judgment because they let their emotions get in the way, and as I have already said there is no greater magnifier of emotions than money. Even if you just have the tiniest hint of greed in you, the share market will bring it out in you. Everybody seems to want to know how to master the share market, but all they really need to know is how to master themselves.

"Before you even think about investing in the share market, you want to be very clear on your desired outcome. You need to decide if you are investing for income or growth, because these are two very different strategies.

"If you are investing for income, you need to make sure that the company is profitable and pays dividends. Dividends are simply the amount that the directors of the company pays out to the shareholders.

"Some people attempt to gain from market movements by short-term trading. If you are going to take the risk of trading, you need to educate yourself considerably on the strategies and techniques of trading. There's the old joke, 'How do you make a small fortune? Start with a big one and trade it in the market!'

"My primary method is to invest for growth. So I invest in quality businesses that I understand, for the long term."

"So," I said, catching on, "before you buy shares in a company, you make sure that you know enough about the business so you can determine what its prospects are?"

"That's right. When you buy shares you are buying a small part of the company. When the company does well, you do well — and when the company does badly, you do badly — so it makes sense that you find a business that you think is going to perform well. The only way you can do that is to only invest in companies that you can understand what the business does and how it intends to do it in the future. It just takes a bit of research!" he said.

"Let's go back to the Three Laws of Money Magnetism: uniqueness, value adding and leverage. Have you found that they have been working in your life?"

"Certainly," I replied.

"And how about in your business?"

"Definitely!" And it was true — my business was certainly doing well now that I applied the Three Laws.

"Well, then, find companies that display all those qualities. A business that have carved out a unique and unmatchable niche in the market. A company that sells products for which it has exclusive or near-exclusive supply, products that customers want and are prepared to pay for."

"So," I said, "if I were going to invest in shares, I want to find a business that has vision and leadership but also has established a strong market presence."

"That's right. It is rare that rich people invest in unproven companies that are not already displaying profits, and yet the greed inside some people often see them taking hot tips on start ups and companies that have not proven themselves. Unfortunately, they pay off occasionally, which just fuels the fire of greed. Far more never pay or take years to pay back the original investments."

"OK, so I want a company that I understand, that demonstrates usage of the Three Laws of Money Magnetism and is already showing a profit," I summarised.

"Exactly. I think you're ready to do some research."

Lesson

Investing in the share market will reveal your true relationship to money. Any error in judgment — whether from greed or hesitation — will quickly be magnified.

But the share market also provides great opportunity for those who have a clear purpose for investing and who select companies that apply the Three Secrets of Money Magnetism, have vision and leadership, and which have established a strong market presence.

CHAPTER 25

The Three Keys to Successful Share Investing

Kevin's office was a hive of activity. People were coming and going, the phones were ringing and business was obviously good.

Kevin was a travel agent whom my wealthy friend had suggested I visit because I was having trouble locating a car that I wanted for my forthcoming Europe holiday. I wanted something special, and all the other agents had just turned up the standard cars through the big rental companies.

When my wealthy friend suggested Kevin's company I was a bit dubious. I had seen their ads on TV and knew they were discounters, and I wondered how they could help me. My wealthy friend assured me it would be worth my while.

I waited about three minutes for Kevin to finish a booking for a customer. He went to great detail to explain to them how the booking worked, what they had to do, how many bags they could take and so on. It was obvious that he was taking a lot of care.

"Big customers?" I asked, when he was done.

"No, not really, just a discount domestic airfare, but the person I booked it for had never flown before and I wanted to make sure she knew everything about it. She's visiting her granddaughter interstate, and I didn't want such an important event ruined by small things a customer wasn't expecting because she hadn't flown before."

I did some quick maths in my head and realised that the commission on the ticket would have been less than $5, and yet Kevin had behaved like the customer was the Queen. I was impressed. Obviously they didn't just pay lip service to the ideal of service here.

I explained my problem to Kevin and apologised for having already booked my flights and accommodation with somebody else. I knew the commission on a car rental booking wouldn't be much, and I was about to ask him to do a fair bit of research for me.

"Well, actually," he said, "it's no bother at all. We have a central research arm of our most experienced consultants. If I didn't know the answer to your question, I could just place one phone call to them and they would. But as it turns out, you are looking for a small company in Switzerland that specialises in this type of rental. They will deliver your car to you anywhere in Europe and arrange to pick it up again when you're done. Can I have a quick look at your tickets to make sure we get the dates right?"

"Of course." This guy obviously knew his stuff.

"OK, well, the dates are correct, but do you mind if I make a suggestion?"

"Not at all."

"If you are prepared to stay one extra day in Europe, it would put your return flight into a different price bracket, which will save you about 20%. And this ticket is booked in 'J' class, which is the most expensive way to do it. I can rebook it another way so you will still be flying Business Class but saving another 15%. Or, if you like, we can leave the price as it is and upgrade you to First Class — would you like me to do that?"

This was the first time I would be flying First Class — how could I refuse? Not only had he just rendered a valuable customer service, he had just scored himself a big commission on a First Class ticket and won me as a customer.

"If you let me have a look at your itinerary, I might be able to make some suggestions on that too. And of course you'll need travel insurance."

An hour later I walked out with a whole new and considerably better holiday, but not before asking Kevin why he was so committed.

"Well," he said, "this business only hires committed people in the first place, but it's more than that. We are constantly reminded of the company's vision; we're constantly trained to within an inch of our lives; every manager and team member is rewarded with bonuses when they perform; and the company is expanding rapidly, so there is lots of opportunity for promotion. We love working for the company and we have faith in the management. They treat us well, which means that we treat the customers well."

And then he said the magic words: "And not only that, the company is giving all of us shares in the up-coming float."

Sheesh, my wealthy friend's a cunning bugger, I thought.

"So what did you think of Kevin?" my wealthy friend asked when we met up again later that week.

"Brilliant. His service was excellent and he made money for the company — that has to be a winning combination!"

"I thought you'd find that. I've been watching this company for some time and it fits the Three Keys to Share Investing: growth, quality and low risk.

"When looking for *growth* you've got to find companies that are increasing their revenues or turnover and their profit. Anybody in business will tell you that it's easy to increase turnover by slashing prices, and it's easy to increase profit by slashing costs, but these are both short-term measures that will eventually run a company into the ground. It takes real talent from a management team to increase profits and turnover at the same time and do it consistently."

"So," I said, "I should be looking for companies that have increasing turnover and increasing net profit."

"Don't forget the share price," said my wealthy friend. "Rich people always wait until the share price is going *up* before they buy. And preferably it should have been going up for quite some time. One of the wealthiest investors in the world once said,

'I have made a fortune by buying too late and selling too early.' What I think he meant by this is that a profit is a profit. It's no good buying a share when it is going down because you think it's cheap. Many people have lost their shirts doing that as the share price continues to go down and down. And if you are going to sell, don't wait until everybody is bailing out; sell when you are happy with the profit. If the share price keeps going up, forget about it. In fact, forget about the share as soon as you've sold it."

"So," I said, "buy shares when they are going up and sell them when they are still going up."

"Yes. And the second part of the formula is *quality*. A quality company is one that is well established with a history of success, makes a product or service that is easily understood by its customers and is in demand with them, and whose management has vision and the competence to carry out that vision.

"There are many huge companies which are low risk because they are run by very competent people, but their management has run out of vision. It is vision that creates uniqueness. Eventually if a company runs out of uniqueness it will run out of steam. For some companies their only uniqueness is that they are huge. This can serve them for decades, but eventually it will catch up with them; in the meantime, their share price won't grow as fast as companies that have competent management carrying out an inspiring vision.

"Another thing to look for in a company is management ownership. Look at Kevin. Do you think he tries just a little bit harder because he is going to be a part owner? Of course he does. Even with a small business, no matter how good staff are, it is the owners who have it on the line so it is they who put in the most effort. It's the same with large companies as well. Look for companies where the directors have large shareholdings. They don't have to have founded the company, although this is often the case, but they must have their own money on the line.

"Be careful to do your research thoroughly, because big companies issue share options to their executives. These options don't cost anything for the companies to issue, so they are technically worthless unless the share price goes up. But because the executives didn't invest their own money, it doesn't really matter what happens as long as they keep getting fat pay packets!"

"So," I said, "I want a company where the management thinks like an owner, and where the directors have high share ownership in the company."

"That's it."

"And finally, let's look at *risk*.

"If a company is too small it can be very hard to get information on it and it's hard to monitor, so make sure you are buying in the Top 500 listed companies.

"One of the greatest risks to a company's success is borrowing. We know that it is easy for enthusiastic people to overreach every now and again. This most often happens when a company borrows too much money and pays too much interest. It doesn't matter why the company has borrowed — although it's usually to expand rapidly — if it has borrowed too much, it will reduce the profits and stop growth.

"Companies that borrow too much are high risk. Even some of the biggest companies on the planet, with great vision and drive, have come unstuck when they have borrowed too much."

"OK, let me see if I have understood you," I said. "To summarise, I want:

- high growth of turnover;
- high growth of profit;
- a consistent increase in the share price;
- an exciting business plan with vision being carried out by competent management;
- high personal ownership of shares by the directors and management;
- one of the Top 500 listed companies; and
- low borrowings and interest costs."

"That's right," said my wealthy friend.

"Where do I get the information from?" I asked, keen to get into it.

"Well, you can start with the companies themselves, as they are required by law to make this type of information available to investors, and it is contained in their annual reports and prospectuses. You can also look in the papers and trade magazines and other publications that make this data available. But remember to formulate your own opinions. Don't give away your knowledge power by trusting other people and then blaming them for your failures or giving them credit for your successes.

"All share-market investments carry a level of risk. If you invest, you are bound to lose money at some stage. Even the best investors have lost money. But they have become the best because they have learnt from those losses and kept investing using the lessons to build their skill.

"Why don't you do the research on Kevin's company and see if it fits the criteria in your summary list?" my wealthy friend suggested.

And of course, as I expected, it did. I bought some shares in the company's float, and some six years later they had grown by over 1000%. I wish I had bought more!

In my experience, quality companies with good growth potential *are* hard to find. Over the years it is rare that more than two or three companies per year will fit my strict investment profile, but when they do come up it is usually well worth it.

Of course, my wealthy friend's prediction that I would lose some money proved correct. Even the best companies sometimes suffer downturns in their share price, and not all of my selections grew in value as I had expected. But in the years since I adopted this approach, I have never had a negative year. I have only ever had one year where *all* the shares I selected grew in price, but most years the ones that did grow grew so dramatically they more than made up for the ones that lost me money.

I keep my shares for as long as they fit my criteria. If the company changes direction into an area I don't understand or I don't think will benefit it, if the management changes dramatically or the directors start resigning and selling their shares, if the growth or profitability disappears, if the company starts borrowing a lot of money or its interest burden gets too high, if the directors start making too many mistakes or errors of judgment, or if corruption or greed sneaks in, I sell.

Most years I have between eight to 12 shares in my portfolio. Some pass my strict criteria and are allowed in. Some I sell, and I have seen my portfolio grow and grow into many millions of dollars. As the companies I have invested in succeed, I have succeeded. As the companies I invested in grew, my wealth grew with them. Some people may have made more money than me over that time, but most have made considerably less.

And I now own shares in some of the biggest and most successful companies in the country and I am proud that I owned them from the time when they were just little.

Lesson

The Three Keys to Successful Share Investing are *growth, quality* and *low risk*. So look for the following:

- high growth of turnover;
- high growth of profit;
- a consistent increase in the share price;
- an exciting business plan with vision being carried out by competent management;
- high personal ownership of shares by the directors and management;
- one of the Top 500 listed companies; and
- low borrowings and interest costs.

CHAPTER 26

The Day I Knew I was Rich

It was a late winter afternoon and I was sitting at my desk when my beautiful friend, who still worked with me, came into my office.

"What a day," she said.

"I know what you mean."

I had been swamped with the trivia of running a business and living a busy life.

"My friend Emma just called," my beautiful friend went on, "she's in France. I wish I were with her."

I stopped for a second and thought, why the heck not?

Plans were hastily laid, passports gathered, and we found ourselves in First Class on the way to Paris.

We picked up a Ferrari and drove down the Côte d'Azur to Nice. I was truly excited to be driving such a beautiful car at high speed down the Auto-route and loved every minute of it.

We checked in to the Hotel Negresco, which is a rather unique luxury hotel that some people say is the best in the world (but I could name many that are better!). The Beatles wrote "The Fool on the Hill" while residing there and a whole host of famous glamour pusses have stayed there. But you can't argue with the service, and the rooms are something to be seen.

My wealthy friend had told me, "Even if you don't like it, staying at the Negresco is one of those things you have to do to know that you have 'made it'!"

The porters wear an elaborate woollen uniform which is splendid to behold but must be ridiculously hot in summer, and people line up to have their photos taken with the strapping young porters who all seem to prefer posing with the pretty young things in bikinis than actually carrying bags!

My beautiful friend and I went on a shopping spree. We had only brought the clothes we were wearing and my platinum credit card (this was one of those holidays where *no* expense would be spared!). For the first time in my life, I went into the most expensive boutiques in the world and indulged myself and my beautiful friend without even asking the price. We could afford it and, after working so hard for seven years, we deserved it! I bought myself a magnificent Italian suit, and her a lovely hand-beaded designer dress.

We booked a courtyard table at La Terrasse de la Salle Empire restaurant at the Hotel de Paris in Monte Carlo, then we dressed in our new finery, and called for the porter to ask the parking attendant to bring up the car.

It was a beautiful night. The moon glistened on the water and the sounds of music and revelry drifted up from the streets.

We went downstairs to collect the car and I happened to stop to ask the concierge where we should park at the Casino.

"Oh," he said, in a rather condescending manner as only the French can muster, "there is no parking there for anybody but VIPs. You would be better off getting a taxi."

"I see," I said, disappointed I wouldn't be able to drive the beautiful Italian car on such an amazing night, "I guess when the car gets here we ought to tell the parking attendant to take it back to the car park."

"Yes, yes, no parking at the Casino — get a taxi," he repeated, just to make sure the silly tourists got the message.

My beautiful friend and I went outside to wait for the car. The night was so lovely that even this disappointment spoilt my mood for only a fraction of a second.

I could hear the Ferrari coming long before I could see it.

Car park attendants in Australia have always driven my Ferrari with reverence (well, at least while I was looking, anyway), but in Europe they consider it an insult for anybody, parking attendants included, to drive such a special car in any way but with gusto, especially when the car is bearing Swiss number plates (a dead give away it is a rental).

The attendant swiftly got out of the car and opened the doors for us. I walked over to the car and stopped next to the open door, soaking in that glorious leather smell and searching in my wallet for the right-sized note to give the attendant a tip while at the same time preparing to send him back to the car park with the car.

It was taking me a bit of time to do the currency conversion, and the attendant said, "Sir is not taking the car?"

"No," I replied, "I am not."

"Why isn't sir taking the car?" the attendant asked, with a look on his face somewhere between greatly concerned for my mental health and pure derision.

"Because the concierge said I would not be able to park it at the Casino."

"Ay ay ay ay," said the attendant before launching off in the direction of the concierge's desk, shouting something in French that I could only assume, by the looks on the faces of the people walking past, was an obscenity.

Instantly the concierge came out with a very worried expression on his face and said, "I am terribly sorry, sir, I cannot believe how stupid I have been. Of *course* they will park *this* car! This *is* a VIP car, sir." And he held the door open for my beautiful friend.

I gave the parking attendant a very big tip.

I had never driven to Monte Carlo before and was worried that we would not be able to find the Casino when we got there (not that the town is all that big, but we were in a foreign country and all), so when I pulled up alongside a BMW 5 series, I asked the driver for directions.

"We are going there now," he said in an accent I couldn't place, "just follow me."

And I did.

The big black BMW turned a corner and there it was — the Grand Casino Monaco, a magnificent 18th-century sandstone building that you have to pay to enter (to keep out the riff-raff).

The square in front of the Casino was very crowded, full of people taking photographs of the rich, famous and beautiful, or ogling the magnificent line-up of parked cars: Rolls Royces, Ferraris, Porsches, Lamborghinis and other assorted exclusive and exotic marques.

The last time I had been here was in the middle of winter, it had been pouring rain and the crowds had obviously stayed away, but even then I added up more than 10 million dollars' worth of cars in that car park. Tonight I guessed there would be over 50 million dollars' worth.

We were inching along towards the square in front of the Casino when the BMW was stopped by a white-gloved policeman. A spirited conversation was had, and the policeman waved the BMW away.

"Goodness," I remarked to my beautiful friend, "the car park must be full. *Now* where are we going to park?"

I now know that Monaco is the most heavily policed state in the world, with surveillance cameras covering every square centimetre. Crime is virtually non-existent and I could have parked the Ferrari anywhere and it would have been safe, but I didn't know that then and I was genuinely concerned for its wellbeing.

We pulled up alongside the policeman to ask him directions, but he just waved us through. Two immaculately dressed attendants rushed to open our doors, and we were in.

All of a sudden it dawned on me what the concierge of the hotel was saying. Even a BMW wasn't good enough for this car park — Ferrari was entry level!

As my beautiful friend and I stepped out of the car, light bulbs flashed and I truly felt like a movie star. They were probably photographing my beautiful friend (who was and is tall, blonde and a former model), but that didn't stop me basking in the glow. I asked the attendant to take a photo of my friend and me in our glamour-puss outfits and in front of the Casino and car.

A parking slip was thrust into my hand and my Ferrari was whisked off to be with friends it hadn't seen since they had been in the factory together. It was sure going to be happy here.

My beautiful friend and I went into the Hotel de Paris and sat at our table in the restaurant, and people were still taking photographs of those of us there. I could tell that the people around us were quite used to it, and my beautiful friend recognised a number of famous faces.

She chose the caviar, and I chose the lobster.

All of a sudden my beautiful friend said, "Oh Peter, you're rich!"

"What?" I said, thinking it was rather gauche of her to point this out in such fine company.

"You're rich! This is what we had said we would do when you were rich. Remember, back in your condemned house when you were working at the supermarket, just after you came back from your first meeting with your wealthy friend. This is what we had said we would do when you were rich!"

She was right. We were at the Grand Casino in Monte Carlo, the most exclusive city in the world; we had arrived in a Ferrari; and my beautiful friend was indeed wearing a $10,000 Dolce & Gabbana dress.

I was rich, and I had the photo to prove it!

My dream came true. May every dream you have come true, too.

Lesson

Dreams can come true if you have the courage to make them happen.

CHAPTER 27

Live Your Dream

The thing I like most about my work is that I get to do what I love each and every day.

Because I chose to do what I love, it led me to wealth. And because my wealth has allowed me to choose what I do, I can wake up and love that I am going to work.

For a long time I could think of nothing more fun than teaching people the secrets to financial freedom through sharing my experience and techniques in seminars. Being a frustrated actor, I loved the idea of getting up on stage and entertaining at the same time as teaching (a colleague later termed it "edutaining").

At first I was reluctant to talk about wealth-creation and at the same time earn an income from teaching it. It seemed to me that as soon as you start saying you are wealthy, other people's natural jealousy starts kicking in and they want to tear you down. I wanted to avoid this, but I had a dream that I would be able to teach people how to be financially free, to give them the choice to live their dream.

A group of friends had me conduct wealth workshops in my lounge room. They had seen how I had pulled ahead of them in wealth while not necessarily working that much harder than they had. Certainly, we all had the same start — if anything, they acknowledged that I started a bit behind.

After some of them were successful, they encouraged me to start presenting wealth-creation seminars. They knew I was a good presenter from attending my business seminars, and in those days there was nobody teaching wealth strategies to ordinary people (certainly nobody without some form of hidden agenda, anyway).

But I didn't want to push it. I thought if I was supposed to be doing it, I just should "let it happen". That way, if the opportunity came up I would know I was on the right track.

One day I was doing a presentation to business owners about how to improve their profits. I got a pretty good reception and, I must admit, I was in good form that day. One of the other presenters didn't show up, so the organiser asked me if I had anything else to talk about.

"How about investing?" I asked.

He checked his schedule and, seeing he didn't have anybody else on that topic, he gave me the OK. It was a one-hour slot leading up to lunch.

I got up on stage and, without having prepared anything, I began telling them the story you have just read. At lunch time, I just kept on going and said that if anybody wanted lunch they could leave and it would not offend me. Only six of the 250 people present left, and four of those came back with bits of the buffet lunch on their plates. Some of the conferencing staff from the hotel had gathered in the back of the room to listen. At the end of my two-hour, unscripted presentation I received the first standing ovation of my life.

I got a lot of positive comments, ranging from "It was obvious that you knew your stuff" through to "I have never heard investing information presented in an interesting and plain-English way before." More importantly, I loved it.

That afternoon a person walked up to me and asked if I presented wealth-creation seminars.

"No, but I would like to," was my reply.

"Then I know somebody you should be speaking to."

And so the die was cast yet again. I was introduced to a gentleman who had a group of clients wanting wealth-creation seminars, and my next presentation was to 850 people. I must admit it sucked a bit, but I was determined to do everything my wealthy friend had taught me to do: create uniqueness, add value into people's lives and find leverage (both for myself and others), and to convince others that they deserve to be wealthy too.

Over the years I have got better and better at what I do, increasing my skills and knowledge and loving every second of it. I have presented my message to hundreds of thousands of people, and the attendance at my seminars grows every year.

No matter what happens in my life, from here on in I know that I am one of the lucky ones — I realised that I deserved wealth, and went and found my way of achieving it.

And if you don't deserve to be wealthy, I don't know who does.

Everybody deserves wealth. It unlocks the door to so many opportunities, so many freedoms, and frees us from so many worries.

If wealth were hard to get I would understand why people didn't go after it, but the strategies I have presented to you are as easy as they sound. And if you have made it this far, you are better than 90% of people who buy books and never finish them.

So many people wait until they are at the end of their lives to do what they love.

My wealthy friend once said to me, "You know, Peter, I used to think I had a lot of time, but I realise I don't. I missed so much of my children's lives working. I look at my youngest. He's 15 and we go sailing together every year. I thought I had heaps of time left to be with him, but now I realise I have just three more sailing trips. When he hits 18, he'll be off to university and starting to build his own life. Just three more times. I've decided to make the most of every second."

Take this opportunity to see yourself for what you are: a high-performance machine that is capable of amazing feats.

Most people are living far below their potential just because they are afraid of being unique, afraid of standing out from the crowd.

My beautiful friend gave me this quote, which I believe sums it up:[1]

---

[1]From Marianne Williamson, *A Return to Love: A Reflection on the Principles of a Course in Miracles*, HarperCollins, New York, 1992.

We ask ourselves, who am I to be brilliant, gorgeous, talented and fabulous?

Actually, who are you not to be?

You are a child of God. Your playing small does not serve the world. There is nothing enlightened about shrinking so that other people won't feel insecure about you.

I suggest it is time for you to take up the challenge. I suggest it is time for you to find your dream and live it. I suggest it is time for you to become the person you know you deserve to be, for yourself, for those you love and for the fullest potential of the Universe.

The strongest message that I have is: "If I can do it, so can you."

How ridiculous was it for me as a check-out operator to imagine the type of life I have today? Yet I dared dream, I dared take action, and I persisted. I didn't give up when things got tough, as they inevitably will.

Most important of all, when people told me that my dreams were ridiculous, I didn't listen to them. I already knew my dreams were ridiculous — what I needed were people who were prepared to help them come true.

One of the highlights of my career was to speak to 18,000 motivated and enthusiastic Australians, in the one venue, about how they could find and follow their dream. I have spoken to larger audiences, but this day will always be special to me.

My wealthy friend introduced me by saying, "Ladies and gentlemen, please welcome a remarkable man, my wealthy friend, Peter Spann."

I smiled and knew that I had "made it". Here I was, just seven short years after working at a check-out where the only person who would listen to me was somebody who had to carry out a price check, speaking to 18,000 people. What an amazing thing, I thought. What a privilege, what an honour.

I marvelled at how my life had once been and what it had become, and every day I thank God for the opportunities I have had.

Living your dream is easy to do, and it is easy not to do. It's your choice.

You don't have to wait until you are destitute, sitting on a broken-down car in the rain, to decide to do something about your financial future. You don't have to wait until the end of your life, when time has almost run out, to decide to live your dream. *You can do it now.*

I have a lot of toys and material possessions, but if I lost all that tomorrow, it wouldn't matter. Firstly, because I know the Key to Wealth and that is knowledge. I know that I could get back the wealth I have today faster than I got it the first time, and with more ease; and secondly, because it is my knowledge and my personal choice that allows me to do what I love.

I often stop at the end of my seminars to sign autographs and talk with people. One night, a man waited until everybody else had left (which took quite a bit of time), and although I was very tired, this man had been patient and had specially asked my personal security man if he could see me at the end.

I must admit I was a bit on auto-pilot. It was very late at night, I had just presented a four-day seminar and signed over 300 autographs, but there was something about him that made me stop and listen.

He introduced himself and quietly thanked me for changing his life, telling me how well financially he had done by implementing the strategies I had presented in my seminars.

I interrupted him and said what I normally say to people at this point, "All I have done is my job. I have just acted as a conduit of knowledge. I did not create the knowledge, I am just privileged enough to have a talent to pass it on. Anything you did, you did for yourself, by yourself and you are the only one who deserves the credit for anything you have achieved."

"Maybe so," he said, "but the other day, as I was running late for a critically important meeting, I noticed that my five-year-old son, the youngest of four, was having difficulty in tying his shoelace. I knew that he'd get it eventually, but he was obviously getting frustrated and upset. I also knew that if I delayed for even a minute I would miss my bus, and that would mean I would miss my meeting. At that moment I had to choose between my son and my job. And for the first time in my life, I chose my son. If it hadn't been for you, I would not have stopped. I realised that in ten years time I would never remember whatever it was that I was on my way to do, but I would always remember my son's *first day* at school."

I love what I do. I love every minute of it, but even though I am well compensated financially for what I do, no amount of mere money could compensate me for the time I give to my work. No amount of money could compensate me for that time out of my life.

But that man's comment, and the hundreds I receive every week, are more than enough compensation for everything I have ever given up in my quest to learn and to share knowledge. And that is my dream — to be a fellow student with you.

Seek the knowledge and skills that will take you to financial freedom. Do it for yourself and for those you love.

I have faith and belief in you.

I know that you can do it.

And when you do, I'll see you there.

CHAPTER 28

Now It's Your Turn!

There are many lessons from my story that will put you on the road to wealth. In this chapter, as in life, there are things to learn, to do, to know and to be grateful for.

Who is in charge of your destiny?

There is only one person in charge of your destiny, and that person is you.

To do: Practise taking control in situations where you would have previously allowed others to make the decisions. This will give you confidence to take control in larger, more important situations.

What is the difference between "rich" and successful"?

"Rich" is just when you have a lot of money. "Successful" is when you are doing what you love and love what you do, when you're surrounded by those you love, and you are rewarded in a manner that suits you.

To do: What would you prefer to be: rich or successful?

Is there an easy way to wealth?

No!

To learn: There is no quick-fix way to wealth. It takes time, effort, knowledge and energy.

What would you do with all that money?

The money itself is unimportant. What's important is what you are going to *do* with it.

To do: Make a list of what you would do if you became rich. Include everything you could need, want or desire, from the trivial (toys and possessions as rewards) to the significant, including opportunities you could take and contributions you could make. This list is a strategy in itself, because it will become your reason for becoming wealthy.

How can you help being ripped off and defrauded, misadvised and misled while on the road to wealth?

The answer is simple: by learning everything you can about your area of interest and by learning about yourself (that is, recognising where your strengths and weaknesses lie).

What is the Key to Wealth?

Knowledge applied is the Key to Wealth. There is no problem that has not already had a solution found for it; no idea that has not had a way to come into reality; no success strategy that has not already been discovered, tried, tested and perfected, that has not been recorded somewhere. All that knowledge is just waiting for you to learn and apply.

To be grateful for: Acquiring knowledge takes time, but it should be pleasurable and is often available for free. You can start on your path to knowledge by visiting your local library.

To do: Find something that you can do well and which really interests you, study all you can about it, develop this knowledge into a skill, and focus on finding a way to be rewarded for doing it.

What if you have a great idea and you are passionate about it, but you can't interest anyone in it?

Think about the signals you are sending to others: are you seen as being nervous or desperate? Like attracts like, and you want to attract others who will react positively to your project. So the more enthusiastic you are, the more interesting to others you become, and people will want to help you.

To learn: What you put out is what you get back, and that is the Key to Success.

How can you learn about marketing yourself?

Start by observing good and bad customer service. Think about the shops you go into and the service providers you deal with. I'll bet you prefer giving your custom to a business where the staff are helpful and enthusiastic, and where you are served with a smile. Selling with a smile is one of the greatest skills a person can have.

To do: Think about how you could best market yourself, to ensure others recognise your skills, knowledge, energy and enthusiasm.

A problem can be a positive thing!

Many people fail to take up an opportunity because all they see is the problem. Every major opportunity is presented with a problem — it's a test to make sure that you are really committed to your idea and that you're on the right track.

To learn: Always keep your focus on the opportunity and persist in finding a way to overcome the problem. Remember, there is no problem that has not already had a solution found for it.

Why is being a successful salesperson so important in wealth creation?

Every time you ask somebody to do something for you, and when you are negotiating a deal, and when you are encouraging others to agree to a project or idea, you are selling.

To know: All you need is something you believe in and persistence, and you will be a successful salesperson.

To do: Develop your sales skills at every opportunity. Read books, take a part-time sales job, have your company send you to courses, negotiate *everything*. Sales skills will serve you well in your wealth creation, and it's easier than you think, if you try and keep persisting at it.

What is the First Secret of Money Magnetism?

When you find a talent, a skill, a product that is genuinely unique, something that people want, will pay for, and can only get from you, you will be writing a ticket for riches.

To learn: Be unique, be memorable in a positive way.

What is the Second Secret of Money Magnetism?

When you find ways to add wealth, health, happiness, love or time into people's lives, you will be rewarded for that.

To learn: Add value to others' lives.

To do: Create a list of ways you can add more value into people's lives in your own work or business. Rewards will follow.

What is the Third Secret of Money Magnetism?

When you apply leverage to a good product or service, it increases the returns and rewards that you get. But if you apply leverage to something that loses money, it will compound your losses.

To learn: Apply leverage wisely.

To do: Using Chapter 12, create a list of the different ways of applying leverage. Then think of three ways you can immediately apply leverage to the different areas of your life, work or business.

They shoot sick horses!

Many a great idea has been dashed on the rocks of poor implementation. Work out a plan before you begin. If others are helping you, be vigilant about their training, motivation and supervision, because skills need to be constantly improved in order for your vision to be implemented and succeed.

To learn: Keep learning and be vigilant, so that your vision never outgrows your skills.

When you are on track and enjoying yourself, things will happen easily

The Universe is always in perfect balance. If you are struggling, check your course to see if you have lost your way and then re-focus on your purpose.

To be grateful for: While you remain on course to your dreams, life will be simple.

The power of coincidence and opportunity

Your brain cannot distinguish between a well-formed idea and reality. Just like your brain, nature cannot distinguish between a powerful idea and "reality" either. Coincidences are nature's way of creating your ideas. Universal Convergence occurs when all the power of the Universe converges on your idea and creates the opportunities, resources, people and situations for your ideas to become reality.

To be grateful for: If you stay alert to life's possibilities, you will notice coincidences and be able to act on them.

You cannot expect change if you do the same thing over and over again, because you will always get the same result.

To be grateful for: Be patient and stay alert. You may not always get exactly what you want, but the Universe will always provide everything you need to carry out your plans.

Facing challenges

Challenge creates the character we need to fulfil our dreams.

To know: Every event, good or bad, is part of our life's path.

Borrowing money

Borrow money only when the amount you will make from the investment will exceed the amount you have to pay in interest and costs.

To do: Master the skill of using borrowed funds properly, to buy assets that will grow in value and return more than the interest you are paying.

The meaning of equity

Let's say you borrow money to buy a house — a good property that is going to grow in value — and you rent it out. As it grows in value, you can use what is called "equity", that is, the difference between what the property is worth and what you owe on it.

To know: Value minus debts equals equity.

To do: Build assets with equity. This builds your net worth and your wealth.

Getting to rich

You'll never be wealthy without putting money aside to invest in quality growth assets. Rich people always set aside money for their investments first and only spend anything they have left.

To know: Income only equals lifestyle — assets equal wealth. When you get to a point where the income you receive from investing far exceeds the amount you spend each year, you will have achieved financial freedom — and you can call yourself rich.

To do: Learn to live on 70% of your income, and put the rest towards accumulating assets that will appreciate.

What you should look out for when investing

There are three key elements of all investments:

- *Growth*: the asset grows in value over time.
- *Income*: the asset produces a cash return in the form of dividends, rent or interest.
- *Risk*: the potential of losing your money.

To know: It is virtually impossible to get all three elements in the one investment. If you go for high growth but low risk, then you will probably have to sacrifice income. If you want income and low risk, then you will probably have to sacrifice growth. And if you want income and high growth, then you will have to accept a higher level of risk.

Is it possible to invest without risk?

No. There is no investment without risk. But if you don't invest, you'll never be rich. As a rule of thumb, the higher the return, the higher the risk.

To do: If you are interested in investing in a particular asset, find out everything you can about it so that you know if the level of risk is acceptable.

What is risk management?

First, don't invest in things you don't understand. It is possible to take a few risks if you do quality research before committing and spread your investments around (for example, some in property and shares, while maintaining a small emergency fund) and only ever place a small amount in investments that are high risk.

To learn: All investments carry risk, and you must learn how to manage those risks.

Leapfrogging strategy in the purchase of investment properties

Leapfrogging allows you to buy a series of investment properties without money out of your pocket as long as you can continue to service the loans, which is done by:

- using equity or cash as the first deposit;
- rejuvenating the property to add value (cosmetic rejuvenation only, such as paint or carpets);
- increasing the rental after rejuvenation;
- having the property revalued;
- refinancing the property to draw on its equity for the next deposit; then
- equity and income will grow over time, allowing you to continually repeat the process.

Learning from your mistakes

It is the law of personal development that we are doomed to forever repeat our mistakes until we understand the lesson they are teaching us.

To do: Analyse your mistakes to discover what lesson they hold for us, and always balance your vision with your skills. Ask others for their insights into the lessons from your mistakes, and be humble enough to accept and learn from this "deliberate criticism".

Your character and the sharemarket

Investing in the share market will reveal your true relationship to money. It is a harsh, bitter, swift and ruthless teacher of human character. Any error of judgment — whether from greed or hesitation — will quickly be magnified.

To learn: Discipline and foresight is the key to investing in shares.

To know: The sharemarket also provides great opportunity for those who have a clear purpose for investing and who select companies that apply the Three Secrets of Money Magnetism, have clear vision and leadership, and which have established a strong market presence.

Investing in shares

Do your research if you are to invest wisely. Look for a company that:

- has carved out a unique and unmatchable niche in the market and has a strong market presence;
- sells products for which it has exclusive or near-exclusive supply and which customers want and are prepared to pay for;
- has a sound business plan and a competent leadership to implement that vision;
- is showing growth in turnover and net profit;
- has a consistent increase in the share price;
- has high personal ownership of shares by the directors and management;
- is one of the Top 500 listed companies; and
- has low borrowings and interest costs.

To learn: Look for companies that display the Three Laws of Money Magnetism (uniqueness, value adding and leverage), and which have the Three Keys to Successful Share investing (growth, quality and low risk).

Watching the share price

It might be tempting to buy when the share price is going down, but who is to know how far it will fall? A rich man once said:

"I have made a fortune by buying too late and selling too early." He would wait until the share price was going up before buying, and would sell when he was happy with the profit. Once a share was sold, he'd forget about it.

To learn: A profit is a profit.

And finally ...

Take up the challenge — find your dream and live it. Seek the knowledge and skills that will take you to financial freedom, and don't let anyone tell you that you can't achieve your dream.

To do: Make your own Wealth Creation plan. Start today. Write it down so that you can monitor your progress from today onwards. And remember to practise saying to yourself: "*I* am in charge of my destiny."

Epilogue

The most common question I am asked is: "Is it a true story?"

The facts presented in this story are indisputable, and the techniques presented as strategies undeniably work. They allowed me to go from working a supermarket as a check-out operator to being on the boards of five companies, owning a multi-million dollar home in Australia's most expensive suburb, and having all the toys and freedom that make up a wealthy lifestyle.

They allowed me to live this life with happiness and joy. And they allowed me to seek my dream and follow it.

I have, however, altered the sequence of some of the events. In other words, not everything occurred in the order in which they are presented in this book and, of course, some anecdotes have been added to make the strategies easier to understand.

My wealthy friend is not one person, but a series of people, mentors, characters, situations, books, seminars, learnings and self-reflection, all of which have helped me develop my technique of investing and living life.

Those friends have always been there for me as I sought knowledge and skills to develop myself and my wealth. And they will be there for you as well.

You will be pleased to know that my beautiful friend is still a best friend. Her support, inspiration, and help in my life caused me to dedicate this book to her.

The second most frequent question I am asked is: "Is Kevin's company real?"

And the answer is yes. It is one of Australia's retail success stories and has grown from a small two-man operation to one of this country's largest companies.

You have my best wishes on your journey to wealth and happiness.

Recommended Reading

* Highly recommended
** A must-have

* Graham J. Airey, *The Property Investor's Handbook*, Wrightbooks, Brighton, Vic., 1998.

* Louise Bedford, *Secret of Writing Options*, Wrightbooks, Elsternwick, Vic., 1999.

** Ken Blanchard & Sheldon Bowles, *Big Bucks! How to Make Serious Money for Both Yourself and Your Company*, William Morrow & Co, UK, 2000.

Mary Buffett & David Clarke, *Buffettology: The Previously Unexplained Techniques that have made Warren Buffett the World's Most Famous Investor*, Rawson Associates, New York, 1997.

Greg Cathro, *Australian Share Market Explained Simply: A Guide for Investors*, Wrightbooks, Elsternwick, Vic., 2001.

* Deepak Chopra, *The Seven Spiritual Laws of Success: A Practical Guide to the Fulfillment of Your Dreams*, Bantam, Sydney, 1996.

** George S. Clason, *The Richest Man in Babylon* (first published in 1926), Penguin, Ringwood, Vic., 1991.

** Natalie Cook & Robert Drane, *Go Girl! An Inspiring Journey from Bronze to Gold*, Hardie Grant, Melbourne, 2001.

* Stephen R. Covey, *The Seven Habits of Highly Effective People: Restoring the Character Ethic*, Business Library, Melbourne, 1990.

Dr Wayne W. Dyer, *Real Magic: Creating Miracles in Everyday Life*, HarperCollins, Sydney, 1992.

Martin S. Fridson, *How to Be a Billionaire: Proven Strategies from the Titans of Wealth*, Wiley, New York, 2000.

Leo Gough (editor), *25 Investment Classics: Insights from the Greatest Investment Books of All Time*, Pitman, Melbourne, 1998.

* Robert G. Hagstrom Jnr, *The Warren Buffett Way: Investment Strategies of the World's Greatest Investor*, Wiley, New York, 1997.

Paul Hanna, *You Can Do It!*, Penguin, Ringwood, Vic., 1997.

** Napoleon Hill, *Think and Grow Rich: The Famous Andrew Carnegie Formula for Money-Making* (first published in 1937), Wilshire Book Co, California, 1999.

* Hans Jakobi, *How to be Rich and Happy on Your Income*, Wealth Dynamics, Illawong, NSW, 1998.

Vivienne James, *The Woman's Money Book*, Anne O'Donovan, Melbourne, 2000.

Robert T. Kiyosaki, *Rich Dad, Poor Dad*, Tech Press Inc, Arizona, 1997.

* Dr Beverly A. Potter, *Finding a Path With a Heart: How to Go From Burnout to Bliss*, Ronin Publishing, Berkeley, California, 1997.

James Redfield, *The Celestine Prophecy: An Adventure*, Bantam, Sydney, 1994.

* N. E. Renton, *Negative Gearing: A Plain English Guide to Leverage for Share and Property Investors*, Wrightbooks, Brighton, Vic., 1998.

* Anthony Robbins, *Awaken the Giant Within: How to Take Immediate Control of Your Mental, Emotional, Physical and Financial Destiny*, Simon & Schuster, London, 1992.

E. James Rohn, *The Five Major Pieces to the Life Puzzle*, Brolga Publishing, Ringwood, Vic., 1991.

* E. James Rohn, *The Seasons of Life*, Brolga Publishing, Ringwood, Vic., 1994.

* Jim Rohn, *Seven Strategies for Wealth and Happiness: Power Ideas from America's Foremost Business Philosopher*, Prima, New York, 1996.

Nikki Ross, *Lessons from the Legends of Wall Street*, Wrightbooks, Elsternwick, Vic, 2001.

* Martin Roth, *Top Stocks*, Wrightbooks, Elsternwick, Vic.

Barbara Sher, *I Could Do Anything If I Only Knew What It Was: Discover What You Really Want, and How to Get It*, Hodder & Stoughton, Sydney, 1995.

* Jan Somers, *Building Wealth in Changing Times*, Somerset Financial Services, Cleveland, Qld, 1994.

* Jan Somers, *Building Wealth: Story by Story*, Somerset Financial Services, Cleveland, Qld, 1998.

** Christopher Tate, *The Art of Trading: A Complete Guide to Trading the Australian Markets*, Wrightbooks, Elsternwick, Vic., 1997.

Christopher Tate, *Understanding Options Trading in Australia*, Wrightbooks, Brighton, Vic., 1997.

Denis Waitley, *Seeds of Greatness: The Best-Kept Secrets of Total Success*, Pocket Books, New York, 1986.

** Noel Whittaker, *Golden Rules of Wealth*, Simon & Schuster, Sydney, 1999.

Acknowledgments

Who could have imagined how much went into writing a book? It's not actually the writing, it's the life experiences!

These acknowledgments are a simple thank you to those who continued to support me, encourage me and believe in me.

A special thank you to my beautiful friend, Leisl Baker, whose love, support and belief kept me going through my darkest hours.

To my mum and dad, who always did their best.

To the wonderful and most dedicated teacher in Australia, Dorothy Devine, the only teacher, ever, to get through to me and really teach.

To Margaret Wells, who had no reason to have faith in me but did anyway.

To Phillip Johnson, my first client, and all my clients along the way. Thanks for believing in me and my sometimes outrageous ideas.

To Natalie Cook, who reminded me that goals and dreams are worth striving for.

To Rob and Sue Jamieson, whose love and dedication to their family act as constant reminder that there is true love in the world.

To Philippa Bond, one of the world's greatest and most inspirational speakers and a true guide and friend.

To all my beautiful friends who put up with me in relationships.

To all my wealthy friends who helped me along the way.

To the teachers, trainers, seminar presenters and authors who have shared their wisdom.

To Ian Low, who was my first manager to truly understand my vision for educating ordinary people to take control of their financial destiny and who, with the help of his team, filled countless rooms with those individuals.

To my amazing team at Freeman Fox, whose dedication and spirit have lifted me to perform at my very best.

To all of my students, graduates and clients who have attended my seminars and workshops — thanks for your amazing support and even more thanks for making my dream come alive by implementing the wealth strategies I teach.

To my business colleagues who make the dream come true everyday.

And a strange but special thank you to all those who didn't and still don't think I can make it — the doubters, the nay-sayers, the cynics and sceptics — you have no idea how much determination and strength you have given me over the years!

And to anybody who has a dream, believes in it and gets out there to make it happen.

About Peter Spann

Basically, Peter Spann is a doer! He started out with nothing and set out to learn everything he could about wealth-creation and success. Through investing and running successful businesses he turned that knowledge into wealth that runs into many millions.

In the process, he has accumulated a wealth of experience. Through trial and error, he has learned what works and what doesn't. And it's this practical experience that he will share with you in Wealth Magic.

And unlike many others...

Peter Spann made his wealth through *investing*. In 1995, encouraged by friends to teach them his techniques he presented his first seminar. Since then, he has presented seminars to more than 250,000 people.

Peter Spann continues to stand out as a uniquely successful, independent source of quality investment strategies.

It is his amazingly practical and simple approach to wealth creation that makes his approach so successful. He breaks down all the complex processes into simple-to-understand, easy-to-implement strategies that are so compellingly simple you practically can't help but do them and become wealthier.

Those strategies enabled him to go from 'broke to multimillionaire' in only seven years and, as his 'Success Stories' (get a free copy by phoning 1800 000 369) prove, these strategies are having a profound impact on many more people.

Entrepreneur, Businessman, Investor, Developer, Trader, International Speaker and Philanthropist

Peter owns a number of successful companies whose primary activities include property development, portfolio management, pharmacy and health care, importing and information technology.

He is a highly successful property developer, options trader and share investor and uses the income from these pursuits to fund his leisure activities which include flying, yachting and motor racing and extensive travel.

He is renowned for his generosity and particularly favours children's charities.

He has been featured in magazine and newspaper articles and on TV.

Peter's overwhelming message is clear: "If I can do it, so can you!"

To join the growing list of people making millions using Peter's strategies call his company Freeman Fox on **1800 000 369** for more information.

High Performance Investment Techniques from one of Australia's Most Respected Wealth Educators - Peter Spann

If you're interested in creating an income stream that will free you from working forever – and if you're interested in creating this income stream fast – then the Wealth Magic series of seminars could be the most intensely challenging and valuable experience you may ever have the opportunity to be a part of.

Peter Spann's company Freeman Fox's presents the Wealth Magic seminars which provide independent investors with an unbiased, quality source of information on property, shares and superannuation to assist them in planning a wealthy future.

The seminars achieve this through a coordinated and graduated program that introduces people to investment strategies that are researched, compiled and devised by multi-millionaire investor, trader and educator, Peter Spann. Since he began educating people about their wealth prospects in 1994, Peter has built a reputation of integrity and innovation in wealth creation.

Plan for the future

Freeman Fox's Wealth Magic seminars are designed to teach you how to invest, how to plan for your future and how to increase the returns and profits from your investments.

They use a combination of strategies that vary from conservative to high leverage. Not only are the strategies fully explained, but so are the risks, allowing you to devise an investment strategy that protects your assets while at the same time increases your returns.

Intelligent Investments

Freeman Fox's Wealth Magic seminars provide their graduates with clear, simple, and highly effective investment and trading strategies that can be easily implemented by the average investor.

The strategies presented at Wealth Magic have been comprehensively tested and refined, originally by Peter Spann himself, then by Freeman Fox's panel of experts in their fields and since by literally thousands of graduates who have successfully implemented them.

You benefit by gaining access to expertly devised strategies at a fraction of the cost it would take to hire them yourself.

Freeman Fox's Wealth Magic seminars package a number of little-known strategies, used and implemented by professional investors and traders, into a format that can be used and understood by ordinary people.

The unique Freeman Fox
7 Steps to Wealth

Step 1 'Welcome to Wealth'

This 3 hour introductory seminar presents an overview of our investment philosophy and strategy.

It is ideal for novice to experienced investors who would like new approaches and a clearer strategy of wealth creation.

Step 2 'Money Magic'

This seminar covers property, shares and superannuation so that you can start to build a quality diversified portfolio of assets that will pave the way for financial freedom.

Step 3 'Instant Income'

Expand your knowledge and increase your returns.

This seminar covers options, leverage strategies, using protected margin facilities and options protection strategies, including hedging. It also covers some higher risk, higher return strategies such as options spreads so you can decide if it is 'right' for you to include them in your wealth strategy.

Step 4 Join 'Wealth Club'

The Wealth Club is exclusively for clients who have graduated from our Wealth Magic educational program.

You will be allocated a 'Wealth Creation Manager' who can tailor the strategies to your individual requirements and work with you to develop an exciting wealth plan for your future.

Step 5 'Super Trader'

If you're interested in the fast paced, higher risk, higher return area of share and option trading, then this seminar is for you.

Step 6 Freeman Fox's Financial Services

To fulfil your requirements for financial services, Freeman Fox has associated companies that offer products designed specially to enhance 'Wealth Magic' strategies. These products and services can be used with, or independent of, our educational programs or 'Wealth Club'.

- **Fox Trade**

  For stock broking can assist you with all equities trades, options trades and margin lending requirements.

- **Freeman Fox Finance**

  For property and investment finance that is feature-packed and at highly competitive rates.

- **Freeman Fox Property**

  For Property Syndicates of clients who pool their funds to purchase or develop blocks of units or town houses;

  A buyer's advocate service, and standard agent style listing secured from the general public.

Step 7 Relax and enjoy your increasing wealth!

The 3 Cornerstones of Wealth Magic's Successful Investment Approach

1.   Build Assets

The wealthy know that quality assets held for the long term are the key to wealth. The Wealth Magic strategy allows for the building of a strong and comprehensive portfolio of quality property and shares.

Held for the long term, these assets build up equity and provide for a stable future for you as an investor. They can later be used to generate an income.

2.   Generate Income

At some stage you may want to stop working or supplement your income from your investments. The Wealth Magic strategy uses income generated through share investment and leverage through basic options strategies to generate income.

3.   Protect

All investment strategies carry risk. The higher the return, the higher the risk, so *all* investment strategies need risk management.

The Wealth Magic strategy presents you with various levels of risk, leverage and the risk management strategies you need to protect your investments. The Wealth Magic strategy also allows for share investments to be protected from downturn by various means, including using options to hedge your portfolio.

The Wealth Magic strategy alerts you to appropriate insurances and other methodologies of providing for debt repayment and a legacy.

The Wealth Magic Approach to Building Wealth and Boosting Income

The wealthy know that they have to take some calculated risks to ensure maximum growth, but also that they need quality risk management strategies to ensure their assets are protected.

The Wealth Magic strategy dictates that you to allocate some of your investments into property, some into shares and a smaller amount into higher-risk strategies. Once you are educated and informed, you can decide what best suits you.

To discover more about this unique investment philosophy contact:

FREEMAN FOX

WEALTH FOR EVERYONE

**PO Box 1335,
DOUBLE BAY, NSW, 1360**

FREECALL:
1800 000 369

WWW.FREEMANFOX.COM.AU

At last! One piece of software carries out all the fundamental and technical analysis you'll ever need...

'Fox Trader'

Simplify all your trading and portfolio management with one of the most powerful technical and fundamental analysis software available in Australia today designed specifically for Freeman Fox clients

FoxTrader is powerful investment software combining:
• Fundamental scanning and charting tools,
• Comprehensive filtering and ranking functionality,
• Alerts (that monitor your shares for you),
• Daily share price updates,
• Daily fundamental updates on direct feed from the ASX,
• Portfolio and reporting,
• Company profiles,
• Watch Lists and more
Source information on the principal activity, directors, dividends paid and buy-back schemes, the background and overview of the company as well as key financials.

Advanced Charting Capability

FoxTrader includes as many as 70 technical and fundamental tools to chart against and it enables you to place multiple indicators on a single chart.

Follow your favourite companies and markets.

Market Scanner

Market Scanner allows you to search the entire market for stocks that meet your investment criteria (for example 'Peter's 3 Stock Investment Criteria'.

Now you can scan, filter, sort and rank data quickly and accurately.

Find companies with robust balance sheets, strong cash flow, solid management and high profitability.

An amazing price!

FoxTrader is one of the most comprehensive Technical and Fundamental analysis software available in Australia today.

And, the good news is Fox Trader costs less that software that only performs half the functions.

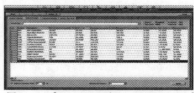

To see a demonstration go to our web site:

www.freemanfox.com.au

and click on the 'Fox Trader' button!

Now you can have Peter Spann "in your home" to tell you everything he knows about wealth creation and becoming rich ...

If you can't attend the "live" seminars, now you can take them home with you to study at your leisure.

You can discover Peter's unique approach to investing through audio, video and the written word.

These programs also allow whole families to share the experience of "Wealth Magic" together.

New titles added all the time

The current list of Home Study programs include:
- Welcome to Wealth (4 hour video, tape & transcript)
- Wealth Through Property (3 hour video)
- Wealth Through Shares (3 hour video)
- Property Magic (7 audio CD's or Tape)
- Shares Magic (7 audio CD's or Tape)
- Money Magic (Video, Audio and Transcript)
- Instant Income (Video, Audio and Transcript)
- Super Trader (Video, Audio and Transcript)
- Millionaire Mastermind (CD's or Tape)
- Life Magic (CD or Tape)

And of course all Home Study Programs come with our 100% Money Back Guarantee

If after viewing the program you are not absolutely convinced that the "Wealth Magic" Home Study Program has provided you with the knowledge, the practical strategies and the confidence you need to become significantly wealthier, just return the program to us for a full refund of your fee. This guarantee is extended for a full 6 weeks from time of purchase to allow you plenty of time to fully experience the program.

Secure your copy now by calling Freeman Fox on: **1800 000 369**

We're happy to answer any questions you have.